The Isles of the Sea

and other West Highland tales

The Isles of the Sea

and other West Highland tales

FITZROY MACLEAN

Illustrated by John Springs

COLLINS
London and Glasgow

First published 1985
Published by William Collins Sons and Company Limited
© 1985 Fitzroy Maclean
ISBN 0 00 435694 2 (standard edition)
ISBN 0 00 435695 0 (special edition)
Printed and bound in Great Britain by Collins Glasgow

Dedicated
With great affection and respect
to

HER MAJESTY QUEEN ELIZABETH
THE QUEEN MOTHER,

who I hope will enjoy
these little Highland tales

A seanachie

Contents

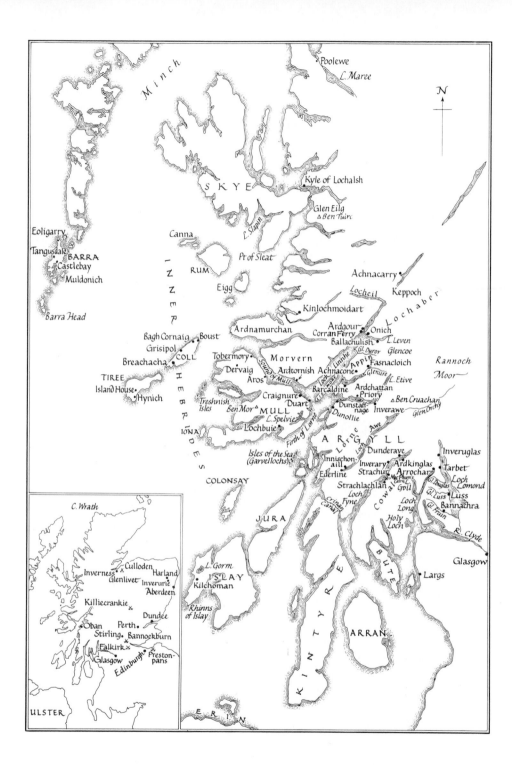

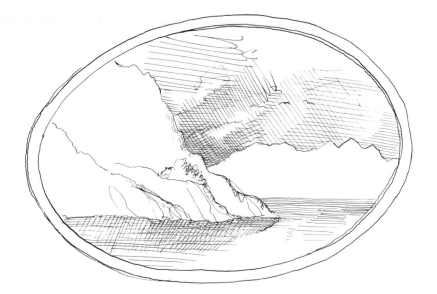

The Western Highlands

THE COUNTY OF ARGYLL in the Western Highlands of Scotland takes its name from the Gaelic *Oirer Ghaidheal,* the Coastland of the Gael. This is where, between the third and sixth centuries of our era, successive waves of Celts from the Kingdom of Dalriada in Ireland landed to establish beyond the sea a second Dalriada closely linked to the first. They were called Scots, or in Latin *Scotti,* being descended, they claimed, from Pharaoh's daughter Scota, who had somehow reached Ireland from the Nile Valley a good many centuries before. In time they gave their name to the whole of our country, which came to be called Scotland. But Argyll and the Western Highlands have remained a Celtic heartland, retaining a quality, a tradition, and, in the Gaelic tongue, a language all of their own.

Twenty miles due west from where I write, the great rock fortress of Dunadd rises steeply from the surrounding meadows. Fifteen centuries ago, this was a stronghold of the newly arrived Scots and capital of Scottish Dalriada. Near its summit you may to this day see, carved out of the living rock, a stone basin and the mark of a human foot. Here, after ceremonial purification, the kings of Dalriada stood to be crowned. Nearby is the carving of a boar, the heraldic emblem of these early monarchs. In the green, hilly countryside around Dunadd carved stones and ancient shrines give a feeling of timeless antiquity. Off the coast, Iona and the other islands of the Inner Hebrides are rich in memories of Columba and those other holy men who brought Christianity to Scotland. While eastern and central Scotland soon fell under Anglo-Saxon and Anglo-Norman influence, Argyll and the Western Highlands, thanks to their remoteness, the ruggedness of the terrain and the native cunning and ferocity of their inhabitants, stubbornly retained their original Celtic character, diluted only by the Viking invasions which, starting in the eighth century, persisted for several hundred years.

Against the Picts of central Scotland, the Scots continued to wage sporadic warfare until, in the year 843, Kenneth MacAlpin, King of Dalriada, having finally defeated them, became, in the words of a chronicler, "the first Scot to rule over the whole of Alba, which is now called Scotia". Meanwhile, in the north and northwest the Norse invaders were fast gaining ground. Soon they had established themselves on the islands and then in the coastal areas of the mainland. Before long they were masters of Orkney, Shetland, and the Western Isles. Caithness and Sutherland followed. In 1098 Kintyre and the Hebrides fell to the Norwegian King Magnus Barelegs.

Resistance to the Norsemen came, when it did, from the part-Norse Somerled, Lord of Morvern, Lochaber, Argyll, and the Southern Hebrides. Somerled, who in 1140 married Ragnhild, daughter of King Olaf the Red of the Isles, did not let his Norse ancestry or connections prevent him from vigorously resisting Norse encroachment or, for that matter, from pursuing his own dynastic interests. Following the death of Magnus Barelegs in 1109, he successfully drove the Norsemen out of Lochaber, Morvern, and the north of Argyll, and in 1156 decisively defeated the Norse King of Man in a great sea battle off Islay. Nor did he show any more respect for King Malcolm IV of Scotland, but sailed boldly up the Clyde, seized Arran and Bute and sacked the town of Glasgow.

On Somerled's demise, his considerable dominions were shared between his sons. True to the tribal system they had brought with them from Ireland, the Scots shared out the territories they had conquered across the sea among families and groups of families. To these were given the name "clan", from *clann,* the Gaelic word for children. From Somerled's elder son, Dugald, who inherited Lorne, Morvern, and Ardnamurchan, sprang the MacDougall Lords of Lorne, whose castles of Dunollie and Dunstaffnage commanded the Firth of Lorne. From his younger son, Reginald, or rather from his grandson Donald, who inherited Islay, the adjoining islands, and part of Kintyre, sprang the MacDonalds of Islay, later to assume the proud title of Lord of the Isles. Such were the origins of two great West Highland clans.

By now the years of Norse encroachment and domination were coming to an end. King Alexander III of Scotland, who came to the throne in 1249, launched a series of raids against the Norseheld Hebrides. In the summer of 1263 old King Hakon of Norway decided to retaliate and set sail for Scotland with a great fleet. Having fought their way ashore at Largs, the Norwegians were heavily defeated on land as well as at sea and withdrew in confusion. Three years later, Hakon's son Magnus signed a peace under which the Hebrides once more became part of Scotland. In practice, however, the Hebrides and large areas of the adjoining mainland remained independent principalities ruled over by the MacDougalls of Lorne and the MacDonalds of Islay, who paid no more heed to their Scottish than they had to their Norwegian overlords.

In the Western Highlands and Islands, more clans were now coming into being, descended either from the Scots of Dalriada or from the Norse invaders: in Cowal the MacLachlans and the MacNeils, later to move to the islands; in Glen Orchy the MacGregors; on Mull the Macleans, those "Spartans of the North", whose name-father, Gillean of the Battle Axe, had fought at Largs; on Loch Fyne the MacNaughtans; on Loch Awe the Campbells, Clan Diarmid, who claimed descent from Diarmid, killer of the Great Boar of Caledon; farther north, the Mackenzies; and near Kyle of Lochalsh and on Skye the Macleods, descendants of Olave the Black, one of the last Norse Kings of Man.

By this time the Norman Conquest of England had added a new dimension to Scottish history. Henceforward, England and her Norman rulers were to intervene increasingly in the affairs of their northern neighbour. With the extinction of the old Celtic line of kings at the end of the thirteenth century, Scotland fell an easy prey to English intrigue and aggression. Ironically enough, it was an Anglo-Norman king, Robert the Bruce, who successfully united the Scots against the English.

It was now that the clans of the Western Highlands acquired the part-patriarchal, part-feudal character they were to keep for the next four or five hundred years. Of those who supported Bruce and were rewarded accordingly, the MacDonald Lords of the Isles were able, following the Norse withdrawal, to establish, with the help of their kinsmen and allies, the Macleans, what amounted to an independent kingdom in the west, embracing the whole of the Western Isles as well as large areas of the mainland. While the Campbells, also supporters of Bruce, now began their relentless ascent to power, the MacDougalls, who had fought against him, suffered accordingly.

Not surprisingly, the Lords of the Isles, desirous of extending their domains still farther, soon found themselves in conflict with the Scottish Crown, which by this time had passed, by way of Bruce's daughter Marjorie, to the likewise Anglo-Norman House of Stewart. In 1411, at the battle of Harlaw, the Royal army, commanded by King James I's kinsman, Alexander Stewart, Earl of Mar, fought to a standstill a host of some six thousand Islesmen who, encouraged by the English, had marched right across Scotland to win fresh territories for the Kingdom of the Isles. Had the Islesmen been victorious, the course of Scottish history could have been different. But although in the end they withdrew without achieving their objective, the Lords of the Isles continued for the remainder of the century to reign as autonomous monarchs from their great castle of Ardtornish on the Sound of Mull.

In the northwest, beyond the Highland Line, what happened in the capital or in the Anglicized south still had but little relevance. Here, the hold of church and state alike was tenuous. A different system, different loyalties, different standards prevailed. The chief was the father of his people. He was, in theory at any rate, of the

same blood as they were. By one means or another he commanded their absolute loyalty. He had power of life and death over
them. His land, in a sense, was their land; their cattle were his
cattle; his quarrels (and they were bloody and frequent) were their
quarrels. In its essence the clan system was patriarchal rather than
feudal, an ancient Celtic concept which bore little relation to the
more recent central monarchy, but had its origin rather in those
early Norse and Irish kingdoms from whose kings and high kings
the chiefs of the great western clans traced their descent.

To the Highlander, land, the wild, barren land of the Highlands; cattle, the stunted little black beasts which somehow got a
living from it and from which he in turn got a living; and men, men
at arms to guard the land and the cattle, were what mattered. The
clan lands belonged by ancestral right to the chief and were distributed by him among the members of his family and the men of his
clan. The cattle were the most prized possession of chief and clansmen alike, the source of their livelihood and social standing and
the source, too, of unending strife. In time of war, the chief and
those of his kin led the clan in battle. When he sent out the fiery
cross, it was the duty of the men of the clan to follow where he led.
The clan had its foundation first and foremost in the deeply rooted
Celtic principle of *kindness,* a mixture of kinship and long tradition,
stronger than any written law. As father of his people, the chief
stood midway between them and God, settling their disputes,
helping them when they were in need, protecting them and their
cattle against their enemies. *Buachaille nan Eilean,* the Shepherd of
the Isles, was a Gaelic designation of the MacDonald chiefs.

With his chief, the humblest clansman shared a pride of race
scarcely conceivable to a stranger. All who bore their chief's name
liked to believe themselves — and often they were — descended as
he was from the name-father of the clan: from Somerled, from Gillean of the Battle Axe, from Calum Mor, from Olave the Black, or
Gregor of the Golden Bridles, and, through them, from countless
generations of Norse and Irish kings. "Though poor, I am noble,"
ran an old and constantly repeated Maclean saying, "Thank God I
am a Maclean". "Almost everyone," the English lieutenant,
Edward Burt, was to write in amazement several centuries later,
"is a genealogist." Little wonder, then, that from their mountain or

island fastnesses the great chiefs and chieftains of the north and northwest, surrounded by their loyal clansmen, should through the ages have paid scant heed to the pronouncements of kings or parliaments or officers of state from south and east of the Highland Line, regarding them only as potential allies or enemies in their own, more personal struggles for power.

None of this made Scotland an easy country to govern. Over the centuries the pacification of the Highlands and Islands was undertaken by successive kings with limited success. On his accession in 1488, the outstandingly able and genuinely well-intentioned James IV seriously tried to make friends of the chiefs of the western clans, hunting and feasting with them, devising useful and supposedly profitable occupations for their followers, and even going so far as to learn Gaelic ("The King actually speaks the language of the savages who live in some parts of Scotland and the Islands," wrote the Spanish Ambassador). But in the end James had to resort to other means. In 1493 the Lordship of the Isles was finally forfeited and annexed to the Crown, and MacCailein Mor, Chief of Clan Campbell and by now Earl of Argyll, appointed Royal Lieutenant of the Isles with full feudal and military powers. Once more, in a time of crisis, the Campbell chief appeared as an active supporter of established authority.

The union of the Crowns under James VI of Scotland and I of England and the consequent disappearance of the English danger in the old sense marked the beginning of a new phase. The seat of power moved south. The Highlands and their turbulent inhabitants were now remoter, less relevant, and more distasteful than ever to their sophisticated Lowland neighbours. To deal with them, James adopted the rough and ready method of issuing Letters of Fire and Sword, by which he authorized one or more clans (usually the Campbells) to deal with their erring neighbours by whatever means they thought best, generally wholesale massacre. In 1609, under the Statutes of Iona, he attempted a more subtle approach, seeking to undermine the clan system by discouraging, without, be it said, much success, such well-established Highland institutions as hand-fasting (a convenient form of trial marriage), the Gaelic language, clan bards and the heavy communal drinking that often accompan-

16

ied their performances, while at the same time seeking to persuade the chiefs to send their sons to be educated in the Lowlands.

From the Reformation onwards and throughout the seventeenth century, Scotland became a prey to almost continuous religious conflict and strife, first between Catholics and Protestants and after that between Presbyterians and Episcopalians, Covenanters and anti-Covenanters. In this, successive Stewart monarchs were personally and inextricably involved, from Mary Queen of Scots to James VII and II. Indeed, it was largely on religious grounds that in 1689 the Roman Catholic James was finally forced to flee the country, making way for his daughter Mary and her Dutch husband, William of Orange. Nor did the hard-fought Battle of Killiecrankie avail to bring him back.

Killiecrankie marked the beginning of the Jacobite movement, sworn to restore King James to the throne. From the first, the Campbells and other Whig clans had rallied enthusiastically to William of Orange; their enemies were predictably Jacobite. Following Killiecrankie, events leading up to the Massacre of Glencoe gave the London government an opportunity to make, with Campbell help, a terrible example of at any rate one turbulent tribe, the sept of Clan Donald who dwelt there.

In the early eighteenth century, two events brought about a revival of Jacobitism: in 1707 union of the Scottish and English parliaments and in 1714, on the death of the last Stewart monarch, Queen Anne, the advent of the generally unpopular House of Hanover, from the first loyally supported by the Campbells. Scotland had now reached a parting of the ways. In the risings of 1715 and 1745 the Jacobite clans were not merely supporting the Stewart claimant to the throne, nor simply striving to get even with the Campbells; they were fighting for something else: for their way of life and the ancient civilization that was part of it. It was this that, with the defeat of Prince Charlie, was irrevocably destroyed at Culloden.

Such, briefly, is the historical background to these tales, which, drawn from a multitude recounted from generation to generation by the seanachies, or tellers of traditional tales, of the Western Highlands and Islands, themselves bear only a marginal relation to history as such. Many conflict with the recorded facts. Others contain an element of the supernatural. In most we need to allow for prejudice on the part of the narrator. Of several there is more than one version and, where this is so, I have simply chosen the rendering which for personal reasons appeals to me most, taking refuge in the convenient Gaelic saying, *Ma's breug bhuam e, is breug chugam e*, "If it be a lie as told by me, it was a lie as told to me". For all that, I hope these stories may help in their way to convey to the reader something of the spirit and frame of mind in which they were told and listened to and something, too, of the wider background against which a number of not unimportant historical events took place. It is even conceivable that sometimes the collective folk memory from which they spring may come closer to the truth than other, more obvious sources.

For all the various tellers of these tales I have used the term *Seanachie*. The clan bard or seanachie, half poet and half historian, was, with the clan piper, chaplain, and physician, an important member of every chief's household, occupying an honoured position in society. His office was, as often as not, hereditary. The stories he told were repeated in much the same words from generation to generation, which gave them the immediacy of an eye-witness account.

Perhaps the most famous bard of the Middle Ages was Muireadhach Albanach. His descendants were to become hereditary seanachies to the MacDonalds of Clanranald. In 1411, Lachlan Mor MacMhuiradhach followed Donald of the Isles into battle at Harlaw, inciting Clan Donald to fresh deeds of heroism, and we learn from James Logan, writing in 1831, that "Lachlan Mac-Neil, *mhic* Lachlan, *mhic* Neil, *mhic* Donald, *mhic* Neil mor, *mhic* Lachlan, *mhic* Donald, of the surname of Mac Mhuirich, bard, genealogist and *seanachaidh* declared before Roderick MacLeod J.P. in the presence of six clergymen and gentlemen that, according to the best of his knowledge, he is the eighteenth in descent from Mhuireach, whose posterity had officiated as bards to Clan Ranald and that they had, as the salary of their office, the farm of Staoligary and four pennies of Drimisdale, during fifteen generations."

Twenty-five years ago, I myself first heard the story of Duncan's Cairn, included in this collection, and of the disastrous battle of Traigh Ghruinnaird, eloquently recounted, first in Gaelic and then in English, by old Donald Morrison from Mull, himself the direct descendant of a long line of storytellers, then on his first visit to the mainland. It was like listening to someone who had himself taken part in the battle. He spoke, I remember in particular, of the basket-loads of severed fingers and thumbs that were picked up on the shore once the fighting was over and the swords and axes had been wiped clean and put away.

Quite naturally, the most important duty of the bard, or *seanachie,* was to celebrate the heroic deeds of the chief and his ancestors. "It was," says Logan, "not only useful to the living to extol the virtues of former heroes as an excitement to their imitation, but was reckoned extremely pleasing to the deceased — it was indeed thought the means of assisting the spirit to a state of happiness and became consequently a religious duty." Not only did the clan bards entertain their chief while he was at table, "rousing his own and his followers' courage by their powerful recitations", they continued their ministrations on the field of battle, where they helped maintain morale, says General Stewart of Garth, by "eulogising the fame resulting from a glorious death . . . as well as the disgrace attending dastardly conduct or cowardly retreat."

Embodying as they did the very essence of the clan spirit, the bards became a natural target for *miorun mor nan Gall,* the Lowlander's historic hatred for the Highlander. The attempts of the Scottish crown to eradicate them, initiated by James VI and I, continued throughout the seventeenth century, with the support of both church and state, as part of a deliberate campaign to destroy the Gaelic, or, as it was called, Irish language, and all that it stood for. Already, before the Union, an act was passed in 1695 for the "erecting of English Schools for rooting out the Irish language and other pious uses", and in 1720 the Society for the Propagation of Christian Knowledge declared their intention "not to continue the Irish language, but to wear it out and learn the people the English tongue".

Nevertheless, the ancient tradition did not die out. In the Highlands and Islands the old tales continued to be told and the old verses recited from generation to generation, and when early in the nineteenth century interest in the Highlands revived, there were still enough storytellers for earnest researchers to be able to find them delighting large gatherings with their tales of long ago.

With the decline of the clan system and the disappearance of official bards, the role of seanachie was assumed by anyone, whatever his station in life, who had a gift for storytelling and a stock of tales to tell. "In every cluster of houses," wrote that great collector of West Highland tales, J.F. Campbell, in 1860, "is some one man famed as good at *sgialachdan* (storytelling), whose house is a winter evening's resort. I visited these and listened, often with wonder, at the extraordinary power of memory shown by untaught old men." Elsewhere he recalls that one of the best and most polished storytellers was a man who had never worn boots or shoes.

In Gaelic there is not the same difference as in English between the spoken and the literary language, and because of the enduring oral tradition, the tales told by the seanachies have at least the same natural liveliness and elegance as written Gaelic records. "When a boy," wrote General Stewart of Garth in 1822, "I took great pleasure in hearing these recitations and now reflect, with much surprise, on the ease and rapidity with which a person could continue them for hours without hesitation and without stopping. . . . It is owing to this ancient custom that we still meet with Highlanders who can give a connected and minutely accurate detail of the history, genealogy, feuds and battles of all the tribes and families in every district or glen for miles around and for a period of several hundred years; illustrating their detail by reference to every remarkable stone, cairn, tree or stream within the district; connecting with each some kindred story of a family or ghost or the death of some person who perished in the snow, by any sudden disaster or by some accidental encounter; and embellishing them with various anecdotes, such topics forming their ordinary subject of conversation."

"In my native place, Poolewe in Ross-shire, when I was a boy," wrote Hector Urquhart, a gamekeeper, in 1860, "it was the custom for the young people to assemble together on the long winter nights to hear the old people recite the tales or *sgeulachd* which they had heard from their fathers before them. . . . I knew an old tailor who used to tell a new tale every night during his stay in the village, and another, an old shoemaker, who, with his large stock of stories about ghosts and fairies, used to frighten us so much that we scarcely dared pass the neighbouring churchyard on our way home. It was also the custom, when an *aoidh* or stranger celebrated for his store of tales came on a visit to the village, for us, young and old, to make a rush to the house where he passed the night and choose our seats, some on beds, some on forms and others on three-legged stools, and listen in silence to the new tales."

Many of the best and most authentic tales come from the Islands, where the tradition of storytelling has lasted longest. "In the Islands of Barra," wrote Hector MacLean, a schoolmaster from Islay in the mid-nineteenth century, "the recitation of tales during the long winter months is still very common. The people gather in crowds to the houses of those whom they consider good reciters to listen to their stories. . . . During the recitation of these tales the emotions of the reciters are occasionally very strongly excited and so also are those of the listeners, almost shedding tears at one time and giving way to loud laughter at another. They speak of the Ossianic heroes with as much feeling, sympathy and belief in their existence as the readers of the newspapers do of the exploits of the British Army in the Crimea or in India."

From Barra comes the first tale in this book, the story of Deirdre of the Sorrows, as told to Alexander Carmichael in 1867 by eighty-one-year-old Iain Donn, Brown Iain, MacNeill. Until thirty years ago this great living tradition was actively continued by the famous John MacPherson of Northbay, better known in Barra and beyond as The Coddy. *"Geurainich Chlann Mhurich,"* runs an old saying, "The MacPhersons and their kin are nimble with their tongues." John MacPherson, a short, thickset, good-looking man, was certainly no exception, being as witty and as articulate in English as in his native Gaelic and endowed with a personality to match.

An Islander born and bred, John MacPherson started life as a herring fisherman and a crofter, and then, in the nineteen-twenties, with money he had saved, he built a boarding house for visitors to Barra, to be known henceforth as *Taighe-an-Choddy*. "This," writes his friend, John Lorne Campbell, who made a collection of his tales, "was the Coddy in his element and at his very best. He was the genial host, the great storyteller and the charming *fear-an-taighe* 'man of the house'." Soon his fame spread far and wide. I am more than grateful to Dr Campbell, himself so distinguished in this field, for permission to use four of the tales the Coddy used to tell, *"Cnoc an t-Sithein,"* "In a Sieve," "The Widow's Cow," and "The Little Witch," the last of these in his very own words, upon which it would, in my view, be impossible to improve. Better than anything, these tales from Barra, springing from a folk memory reaching back a thousand years or more, convey with astonishing immediacy the continuing presence, side by side with our own, of another, supernatural world, of beings liable to intervene every now and then, sometimes for better, sometimes for worse, in our humdrum everyday affairs.

In conclusion, my warm thanks are due to MacCailein Mor, the Duke of Argyll, for authority to draw on the published portion of the Dewar Manuscripts in which he holds the copyright. We owe a great debt to his family over the last century for what they have done to preserve and encourage the bardic tradition in the Western Highlands, and it is good news that he has now authorized the publication of the remaining tales, collected many years ago for the eighth Duke by John Dewar, a Gaelic-speaking woodman from Rosneath.

Strachur, Argyll
August 1985

Deirdre of the Sorrows

A THOUSAND YEARS or more ago there lived in Erin a worthy and prosperous man known, from his skill with the harp, as *Calum Cruitire*, or Calum the Harper. Though long married, Calum and his wife had no children. When they were already well advanced in years, they received a visit from a *fiosaiche*, a seer or soothsayer.

"Are you making soothsaying?" asked Calum Cruitire.

"I am making a little," said the soothsayer. "Might you perhaps be in need of soothsaying?"

"Well," said Calum, "I would not mind taking soothsaying from you if you had soothsaying for me and would be pleased to make it."

"Well," replied the soothsayer, "I will make soothsaying for you." And he went out of the house to take counsel with himself.

When the soothsayer returned, he asked Calum whether he had ever had any children.

"Well, no," said Calum, "We have never had children. Nor can we expect any now; we are too old. There are just the two of us."

"That surprises me very much," said the soothsayer, "for in my augury I see much blood spilled, more than has been spilled in Erin for generations, and all on account of a daughter of yours. And the three greatest heroes in the land shall lose their lives because of her."

"Is that the soothsaying you are making for me?" said Calum angrily, thinking the soothsayer was mocking him. "Because if it is you can keep it for yourself. Neither you nor your soothsaying are worth anything."

"Well," said the soothsayer, "be sure of this: I see it all very clearly in my augury."

"But none of this can come to pass," said Calum. "My wife and I are already old. We can never have a child." And he let the soothsayer go and gave him no reward.

Now not long after the soothsayer had made his prophecy, Calum's wife found to her surprise that she was pregnant. And the heavier she became with child, the more dismayed Calum became, for now he believed everything the soothsayer had foretold. So he decided that, if a daughter were to be born to them, he must at once send her away secretly to a far-off place, where no eye would see her and no ear catch a sound of her, in order that none of the terrible things prophesied by the soothsayer should come to pass.

In due time Calum's wife was indeed delivered of an infant girl, and Calum would allow no one to come to his house save only the *bean-ghlùin*, the knee-woman or midwife. Now deeply troubled, he asked the knee-woman if she would bring up the child herself and keep her hidden for him. And when the woman, whose name was Lavarcham, agreed to this, Calum took three men to a far-off place among the mountains and with their help hollowed out a dwelling within a green hillock. To this hidden sheiling among the great hills Calum Cruitire secretly carried off the child and the knee-woman and there left them with enough food and clothing for a year. And each year, for as long as he lived, he sent them fresh supplies. And they called the child Deirdre, which means "sadness".

For fourteen years Deirdre lived with Lavarcham, her *muime,* or foster-mother, in their lonely sheiling among the high hills, where the *muime* taught her all she herself knew about the birds and the flowers and the trees. With the years, Deirdre grew to be tall and slender and fairer than any maiden in all Erin. But no one knew of her for, true to her vows, the *muime* carefully kept her from seeing or meeting her fellow men.

Then, one wild winter's night, a hunter, lost among the hills and tired and cold, lay down to rest beside the green knoll beneath which they lived, and there fell asleep. As he slept, he dreamt that this was the Hill of the Fairies of which he had often heard, and he called out in his sleep to be admitted. Hearing his voice, Deirdre asked Lavarcham what it was.

"It is nothing," the *muime* replied, "but the birds of the air seeking one another. Let them fly away to the trees of the forest."

Then the hunter again called out in his dream, begging in the name of God to be let in. And again Deirdre asked what it was, and once more was told that it was nothing but the birds of the air crying to one another.

"But I heard the bird beg in the name of God to be let in," said Deirdre. "You yourself have told me that whatever is asked of us in God's name must be done, and I believe you. I will let in the bird." Then, unbarring the door of the sheiling, she called in the hunter, and, seeing that he was cold and hungry and thirsty, gave him food and drink and a place to sit by the fire.

But when the hunter saw Deirdre, he immediately forgot how cold and hungry he was. "Were certain people to see the maiden you are hiding here," he said to the *muime*, "they would not leave her with you for long."

"Keep your mouth shut," replied the old woman.

But Deirdre's interest was aroused. "What people are these of whom you speak?" she asked the hunter.

"I will tell you," he replied. "They are Naois, the son of Uisne, and his two brothers, Aillean and Ardan."

"And what," she asked, "are they like?"

"Their hair," he replied, "is as black as the raven's wing and their skin as white as the swan. They are as strong and agile as the salmon in the stream and the stag on the hill. And Naois stands a full head and shoulders taller than any other man in Erin."

"Be they as they may," said the *muime*, "get yourself out of here and be on your way. It was a black day when Deirdre let you in."

Thus dismissed, the hunter went his way. And, as he went, the thought came to him that Conachar, King of Ulster, was, as the Seanachie puts it, "rising up alone, without a confidential love, without a conversational mate beside him." And it occurred to him that if Conachar were to see Deirdre, he might well decide to take her home with him, which could be to the advantage of all concerned, himself included.

The hunter went straight to King Conachar's palace. "I have," he said, on being admitted to the royal presence, "seen the loveliest maiden in all Erin."

The King was intrigued. "Will you," he asked, "guide me to the place where she dwells? I will make it worth your while to do so."

"Well, I might," said the hunter obliquely, "though my doing so may not be wished."

The very next morning King Conachar rose before dawn, and, taking with him the hunter and his kinsmen, the three heroic sons of Fearchar, son of Ro, set out in search of the green, sunny sheiling in which the lovely Deirdre dwelt. The way was long and the going was rough, and by the time they came to where the sheiling was they were footsore and weary. "There it is now, down on the floor of the glen," said the hunter. "For my part, I will go no nearer to the old woman than this." And he turned back. But Conachar and his companions went down to the sheiling and knocked loudly at the door. For all their knocking, the *muime* would not open the door.

"Open," said Conachar, "and you will get a better house than this, when we get home."

"I am not wanting a better house than my own little bothy," replied the *muime*.

"Unless you open your door willingly, we will open it by force," said the King, who was growing angry.

"Then tell me who is it who is seeking entrance?" she asked.

"It is I, Conachar, King of Ulster," replied Conachar impatiently. At which, in great awe, the old woman opened the door and admitted Conachar and as many of his followers as there was room for.

"When the King saw the damsel who was before him," says the Seanachie, "he thought to himself that never had he seen a maiden as lovely as Deirdre. And he gave her the whole weight of his heart in love." Deirdre was at once hoisted on to the shoulders of Fearchar's brawny sons and, with the *muime,* carried off to King Conachar's splendid palace.

Because of his great love for her, Conachar wanted to marry Deirdre immediately. "But Deirdre," says the Seanachie, "would not do it at all, at all." She had, she said, never been with people before and had no knowledge of the duties of a wife or indeed the manners of a maiden. If he would but grant her a year's delay, she would marry him at the end of it. Accordingly, King Conachar provided her with a teaching woman and some merry, but elegant and modest maidens to be her companions. And the more the King saw of Deirdre, the more she pleased him.

One sunny day when Deirdre and her maidens were out on the hillside, they saw three travellers approaching. As the men came closer and Deirdre could see them clearly, the words of the hunter came back to her, and she knew that these were the three strong sons of Uisne and that the tallest and most handsome must be Naois. The brothers were passing on their way without even glancing at the maidens, but when Deirdre saw Naois, there came to her a feeling she had never felt before, and she knew that she must follow him wherever he went. So, getting up, she left her attendant women where they were and set out after the brothers.

Seeing her and knowing she was the bride of their kinsman, King Conachar, and fearing for their brother, Aillean and Ardan urged Naois to walk faster, saying that they had a long way to go before nightfall. But Deirdre called out after Naois, "Naois, son of Uisne, do you want to leave me behind?"

"What is that cry I hear," Naois asked of his brothers, "which is hard for me to answer and hard to reject?"

"It is but the cry of Conachar's grey geese," replied his brothers. "Let us be on our way."

But Deirdre called after him a second and a third time, and the third time Naois said, "That is a cry of distress. As a hero, I cannot go any farther without seeing whence it comes."

And when they met, Deirdre kissed Naois three times on the lips and each of his brothers once. Then Naois set Deirdre high on his shoulders, and calling on his brothers to walk still faster, set out for the coast, for he knew that he must not now remain in Erin.

When they came to their galley, Naois and his two brothers set sail for Alba, taking Deirdre with them. And in Alba Deirdre and Naois and his two brothers lived happily together in a tower on the shores of Loch Etive in Argyll, the Coastland of the Gaels, where they could kill the salmon in the river and the deer on the hill. And to this day the place where they lived is known as *Dun Mac Uisneachan,* the Fortress of the Sons of Uisne.

By now the year had gone by at the end of which Deirdre was to have married Conachar, and Conachar was planning a great banquet. To his many kinsmen all over Erin he sent messengers bidding them to the banquet. But to Naois and his brothers, who were his cousins, he sent, with malice aforethought, his uncle Fearchar MacRo, who was also their uncle, as a special envoy to tell them of the banquet and ensure that they came to it. For it was Conachar's purpose, once he had lured Naois back to Erin, to take Deirdre away from him by force, whether they were married or not. And when Fearchar reached Alba, his three nephews made him welcome and unsuspectingly accepted Conachar's invitation. Only Deirdre had doubts, which she voiced in song:

> I see Conachar thirsting for blood,
> I see Fearchar full of guile,
> I see Three Brothers lying prostrate,
> I see Deirdre weeping, weeping.

But Fearchar still urged them to go. "For my own part," he said pointedly, "I have never liked and never yielded to the howling of dogs nor to the dreams of women. Conachar has sent you a friendly invitation. It will be unfriendly if you do not come. My three sons and I will protect you." So the sons of Uisne set out for Erin, and Deirdre, with grave misgivings, went with them.

When Conachar heard that Naois and his brothers and Deirdre had landed in Ulster, he gave orders that they were to be lodged in a building filled with a great number of mercenaries. And when the mercenaries saw the sons of Uisne arrive, they laughed out loud, but Naois laughed back, louder than all of them. Then Naois asked the commander of the mercenaries why he and his men were laughing. "Because," the chief mercenary replied, "I have never seen men I would sooner make a meal of than the three of you. And now tell me, you great hero, what were *you* laughing at?"

"I was laughing," said Naois, drawing himself up to his full height, "because never in the whole of my life have I seen men whose heads I would sooner knock off." Whereupon, suiting his actions to his words, he and Ardan and Aillean set about the mercenaries, and, starting with the commander, killed every one of them. Then he and his brothers and Deirdre cleaned out the building, lit a big fire and, says the Seanachie, "were comfortable enough till morning."

Next morning, Conachar, more determined than ever to win back Deirdre and rid himself of Naois and his brothers, sent three hundred more warriors down to where they were, then another three hundred, and then three hundred more. But the sons of Uisne, bravely helped by Fiallan Fionn, their cousin and the youngest of Fearchar's three sons, who alone of the three was true to his father's promise to stand by them, somehow managed to fight off the warriors. All day long they fought, and all night, until, just before first light, Naois said they must go, and together they set out secretly for the place where they had left their galley.

When he learned of this, King Conachar addressed himself to his personal Druid, Duanan Gacha Draogh. "I have spent great sums, Duanan Gacha Draogh," he said, "on having you educated and trained as a Druid and initiated in all the druidical secrets. And in spite of this, these four are now leaving the country without any regard for me whatever and without my being able to prevent them."

"Leave it to me," said the Druid confidently, "I will turn them back." And he caused a dense forest to spring up in front of them. But the Children of Uisne passed clean through the wood, Naois leading Deirdre by the hand. And again Conachar complained of their lack of respect for him.

"Now I will try something else," said the Druid. And this time he caused the grey waves of the sea to flood the grassy plain that lay before them. But Naois lifted Deirdre on to his back and with his two brothers waded through the waves of the sea.

"That was better," said Conachar, "but still not good enough. These creatures continue to show no respect for me."

"We will try something different," said the Druid. And he froze the waves of the sea into jagged hillocks of ice. It was bitterly cold, and, as the children of Uisne struggled through this icy wilderness, Ardan became exhausted and called out that he could go no farther. Naois took Ardan on to his shoulders and carried him, but it was by now of no avail: before long Ardan died. Next, Aillean said that he could go no farther, and Naois bid him cling to him and he would bring him safe to land. "But soon," says the Seanachie, "the weakness of death came upon him and his hold relaxed." And when Naois saw that the two brothers he loved so dearly were dead, he lost any wish to live. His heart was broken, and he too died amid the waters of that frozen sea, leaving only Deirdre still alive.

"I have done what you asked me to do," said Duanan the Druid to King Conachar. "The children of Uisne are dead and will trouble you no more, while your wife-to-be is hale and hearty."

"Well done, Duanan," replied the King. "I no longer regret the money I spent on you. Now dry up the sea, so that I may behold Deirdre."

When the sea had been dried up, they saw the three brothers lying lifeless on the smooth, green turf, with Deirdre bending over their bodies, weeping bitterly. The king gave orders for a grave to be dug and for the sons of Uisne to be buried in it side by side. And when the bodies of the three brothers had been laid in the grave, Deirdre cried out to them:

> *Nan robh ciall aig marbh,*
> *Dheanadh sibhs' aite dhomhsa*
> If the dead had understanding,
> You would make room for me.

Then she lay down in the grave next to Naois, and she too died.

Seeing this, King Conachar ordered that Deirdre's body be taken from the grave and buried on the other side of a little *lochan*. This was done, and the grave filled in, but soon a young pine tree grew out of Deirdre's grave and another from the grave of Naois, and the branches of the two pine trees twined together above the waters of the little *lochan*.

The Story of Diarmid and the Great Boar

TO THIS DAY, Clan Campbell confidently claim as their progenitor the great hero Diarmid O Duibhne who, more than ten centuries ago, performed prodigies of valour in Erin and Alba. For this reason, they are sometimes known as *Siol Diarmid,* the tribe of Diarmid.

Now Diarmid O Duibhne's mother was sister to Fionn Mac-Chumhail or Finn MacCoul, a chieftain of high estate, famous as leader of the Fians, a noble band of warriors, every one of them a hero. In time, young Diarmid, a handsome sturdy lad, grew up, like his uncle Fionn, to be famous even among the Fians for his courage, his sagacity, and his fleetness of foot, all valuable qualities in battle, or indeed in most other situations. Soon he was reputed to be third bravest of all the Fians.

Besides being a hero, Diarmid loved women and was greatly loved by them, being known as *Diarmid Buidhe nam Ban* or Yellow-Haired Diarmid of the Women. This was due not only to his good looks and engaging manners, but also to *ball-seirc,* a kind of beauty spot or love mark high up on his left temple, which, when revealed, immediately caused any woman who happened to be at hand to fall passionately and desperately in love with him. In order to save himself from unwanted entanglements and to have more time for fighting and hunting and other such manly pursuits, Diarmid took to wearing for the greater part of each day a close-fitting helmet which effectively covered up his love mark.

By the time Diarmid had reached manhood, his uncle Fionn, to whom he was devoted, was starting to look round for a wife. Being no longer in his first youth, he was much concerned to pick a wife who would be suitable in every way, and accordingly drew up a list of searching questions for his would-be betrothed to answer. Only one maiden could answer them all: Grainne or Grania, the lovely daughter of Cormac O'Coulin, Earl of Ulster. Most of the questions, and most of Grania's answers, have long been forgotten, but some, still remembered, are revealing. To the question, what is hotter than fire, her immediate answer was, a woman's reasoning betwixt two men. Asked what is quicker than the wind, she replied, a woman's thought betwixt two men. What is the best jewel? A knife. What is blacker than the raven? Death. But Fionn was pleased by her answers, and preparations for the wedding in his castle went ahead.

It was the finest wedding there had been in Ulster for years. All the nobility and gentry of Erin were bidden to the wedding banquet, which lasted for seven days and seven nights. The Fians were great hunters, and after the wedding guests had finished eating, they held a special banquet for their hounds. As can be imagined, there was much snapping and snarling. Then all at once a savage fight broke out between two great Irish wolfhounds which started to tear at each other's throats. Resourceful as ever, Diarmid knew what to do. Throwing himself boldly into the *mêlée*, he dragged the two great hairy brutes apart by main force. But in the struggle his helmet fell to the ground, revealing, for all to see, not just his fine shock of yellow hair, but there, high up on his left temple, *ball-seirc*, the love mark.

Hurriedly, Diarmid replaced his helmet, glancing nervously as he did so at a nearby group of simpering bridesmaids. Much to his relief, they had been too busy with their own affairs to notice anything. Then, right down the length of the great hall, he suddenly caught the eye of lovely Grania, now his aunt by marriage, and knew at once that the love mark had taken effect.

Diarmid's predicament was disturbing. His uncle was dear to him; had brought him up from boyhood; and, as leader of the heroic Fians, was someone he could ill afford to antagonize. Grania he hardly knew. With her great mass of auburn hair, her green eyes, and her slender yet voluptuous body, she was, it is true, beautiful enough for anyone, and much of an age with himself. Until now he had been looking forward to a happy, perhaps even mildly flirtatious, relationship, as between nephew and aunt, but he knew *ball-seirc*. He knew the devastating passions it aroused and the trouble it had given him before, and his heart sank.

Their first encounter came that same evening when Grania sought him out in one of the corridors of Fionn's great castle. "You must take me away with you this very night," she whispered hotly, and Diarmid felt her body move against his in the darkness.

"That I cannot do," he said, drawing away from her, and then added, a trifle lamely, "You see, I love my uncle."

At that moment a door opened farther down the corridor, and greatly to Diarmid's relief Fionn himself came out. For the time being the situation had been saved, but Diarmid knew instinctively that this was only the beginning. Worse still, thinking back on that brief moment in the draughty corridor, he also knew all too well that his own passions were now aroused, that he desired Grania as much as Grania desired him.

Next day, to salve his conscience as a hero, Diarmid sought to put a spell on Grania. He could not be certain it would work. In fact he rather hoped it might not. But he must at least try. Leading her to a quiet corner of the castle gardens, whither, needless to say, she readily accompanied him, he duly repeated the spell to her as it had been repeated to him by a knowing old warlock. "I will not," he said, "take thee without. I will not take thee within. I will not take thee on horseback. I will not take thee on foot. I will not take thee at night. I will not take thee by day. I will not take thee clothed. I will not take thee unclothed." After which, having delivered himself of his spell, he moved with his two favourite hounds into a little bothy not far from Fionn's castle, where he could be alone.

He did not remain alone for long. In the dusk of the evening, betwixt night and day, the door of the bothy opened, and there was Grania on the threshold, halfway in and halfway out. It could not be said she was clothed, nor strictly speaking naked. What she wore was an almost transparent shift of *canach an t-sleibh* or mountain down, which had been made for her by a fairy woman of her acquaintance and which effectively revealed rather than concealed her very considerable charms. Nor, for that matter, was she on foot, or indeed on horseback, for she sat boldly astride an enormous he-goat, in a posture which, in the gloaming, still further

heightened both the wantonness of her appearance and its effect on Diarmid's senses. Hero though he was, he knew when he was beaten. His uncle was forgotten, the goat was hurriedly tethered to a handy ring by the bothy door, and Grania silently dragged inside.

They woke next morning to the realization that, whatever else they might now do, they could not remain where they were. Already, barely a mile away, Fionn MacCumail, missing Grania, would be calling up and arming the Fians and setting out in hot pursuit. And Fionn and the Fians, when roused, were a formidable force. Accordingly, rising hurriedly from the couch where they lay embraced and clothing themselves as best they could in what came first to hand, they flung themselves on to two of Diarmid's fleetest horses and plunged headlong into the sheltering depths of the great pine forest, which in those days covered much of Ireland and most of Scotland. Only the he-goat, by now a little fretful, remained at the bothy to bear the brunt of Fionn's outraged feelings.

"There is no place to which we may go," said Diarmid despairingly, "where Fionn will not find us when he touches his tooth of knowledge. And he will kill me for going with you."

"We will go to Carraig," replied Grania. "There are so many Carraigs that he will never know in which we might be."

So they took ship and went to *Carraig an Damh,* the Rock of the Stag, across the sea in Kintyre. But soon Fionn's pursuit caught up with them, and they had to move on. Their flight took them through much of Alba and on to the Inner and Outer Hebrides. They hid in the forests, among the branches of trees, in any bothies they could find, or in caves by the sea shore.

One night, while they were sheltering in a cave at Kenavara on the Isle of Tiree, which is still pointed out as one of their hiding places, it was so stormy that Diarmid took refuge at the back of the cave, leaving Grania, who rejoiced in the howling of the gale, to sleep near the entrance. But that very night, as it happened, through the storm, a wild and wanton old man called *Ciuthach Mac an Doill*, Ciuthach, Son of Darkness, came ashore from a two-oared coracle, and finding Grania at the entrance to the cave, he threw himself upon her. Nor was Grania indifferent to him. Indeed, she called out to Diarmid, still asleep at the back of the cave, mocking him and saying that, although she had spent many nights with the third bravest man amongst the Fians, she had never until now known a lover like this. Whereupon Diarmid, wakened by her taunts, rose up in his wrath and grappled with the old man and, after a fierce struggle, for the old man was wiry and strong, drove his spear right through him. And in his death throes Mac an Doill gave a terrible shriek which echoed through the recesses of the cave and out across the storm-tossed sea.

Continuing their flight, for there could be no turning back, Diarmid and Grania reached Glen Eilg, across the sea from the Isle of Skye. Now it so happened that at this time Fionn and the Fians had come to Glen Eilg to hunt the wild boar and in a thicket found foot marks which Fionn could see were his nephew's. But the Fians would not believe him, saying that by now Diarmid must surely be dead.

"We will shout *'Foghaid'*, said Fionn, "the hunting cry of the Fians, for that, wherever he may be, he is sworn to answer." So they cried *"Foghaid,"* and Diarmid heard them.

"Do not answer, Diarmid," said Grania. "It is but a trap." But Diarmid answered, as he was bound to, and went down to the shore where Fionn and the Fians awaited him. But when Fionn saw him he could not bring himself to lay hands on his sister's son. Instead, he invited him to join the hunt.

The beast they were hunting was the Great Boar of Caledon, a gigantic beast famed far and wide for its ferocity and for the damage it had done. And Diarmid, happy to be among his former comrades, hunted the great boar up and down Ben Eidin and Ben Tuirc, and in the end brought it to bay at the head of a narrow glen.

With its sharp tusks and enormous bulk, it was a formidable adversary. Even Diarmid's famous sword, forged for him by the great swordsmith Con MacLiobhain himself, was of little avail against the monster's savage onslaughts. "His tempered blade," says the Seanachie, "twisted like a withered rush." With ferocious thrusts of its sharp tusks the boar had by now killed both of Diarmid's hounds. At last, in desperation, Diarmid closed with the boar and, summoning all his energy, somehow managed to drive his spear deep into the great brute's belly. Whereupon, with a last savage grunt, the Great Boar fell to the ground in its death agony.

Watching the hunt, Fionn had half hoped that the boar might do his work for him. But his nephew was still alive and as slayer of the Great Boar, now more of a hero than ever. Heedlessly, Diarmid had taken off his helmet to mop his brow, thus revealing *ball-seirc*, and Grania, regardless of her husband's presence, was even now clinging adoringly to him.

By this time the Fians were arguing, as sportsmen will, about the size and weight of their quarry, which lay where it had fallen like a great, black upturned boat. Then one of them, who had no love for Diarmid, said, "Why does not Diarmid, the great hero, try measuring the boar by pacing the length of its back from end to end?" And Diarmid, pacing the boar's back from snout to tail, measured it and declared that its length was sixteen feet. But then the Fian, who knew the boar's bristles were poisonous and knew the lie of them on its back, called out to him to measure it again.

This time Diarmid paced the boar's back the other way, from tail to snout, against the lie of the bristles. As he paced it, one of the bristles ran into his foot, and he knew at once that he was poisoned. Falling to the ground in agony, he called out to Fionn, his mother's own brother, to help him.

In spite of himself, Fionn pitied his nephew. "How can I help you?" he asked.

"I could be healed by a draught of water from your hands," replied Diarmid.

Fionn went to the spring to fetch the water, but as he was returning with it in his hands, he thought of Grania, and his hands shook with rage, and he spilled the water. Then he thought of Diarmid and was sorry for him and went back for more. But before Fionn could reach him, Diarmid died, and as he died he gave a terrible shuddering shriek.

"Is that not the hardest cry you ever heard?" Fionn asked Grania. "No," she replied coolly, remembering the old man in the cave, "When Diarmid killed him, Ciuthach's shriek was harder." "And," says the Seanachie, "the Fians took Grania and burned her on a faggot of grey oak." And she, too, shrieked as the flames licked fiercely around her shapely body. "And in the same mound as the wild pig," runs the refrain of the famous Lay of Diarmid, "we buried Grania, daughter of Cormac O' Coulin. And the two hounds. And Diarmid."

*　　*　　*　　*

From Diarmid, the Campbells derive their crest of a boar's head. Just how the Dukes of Argyll and their clan are descended from Yellow-haired Diarmid of the Women, history does not relate. But, writing in 1859, a certain Mary MacTavish, a recognized expert on the subject, adds her own gloss to the tale. "I never heard," she declares, *"who* his wife was, but she was esteemed a virtuous and worthy person." The MacTavishes, as is well known, are a sept of Clan Campbell and justly proud of it.

Eilean Fraoch

FROM THE DEEP AND ICY WATERS of Loch Awe among the green hills of Argyll rises an island which bears the name of *Eilean Fraoch*. Some say that this simply signifies the Isle of Heather, others that the name comes from the hero Fraoch. Of Fraoch, they tell the following tale.

Fraoch, Son of Fiadhach, was as brave as he was handsome and as generous as he was brave. His hair, says the bard, was as black and as glossy as the raven's plumage. His eyes were blue, his skin whiter than the driven snow, and his lips, which women longed to kiss, as red as the mountain raspberry. His shield was as wide as a door, his spear as long as a steering pole, and victory smiled on him wherever he went.

Being so brave, so strong, so handsome and, above all, so successful, Fraoch could have won the favours of almost any of the maidens who dwelt in the fair land of Argyll, the Coastland of the Gaels. But he loved only one, beautiful Morag, daughter of Corul of the Generous Cups, a chieftain known far and wide for his lavish hospitality, and of Corul's lovely wife, Maeve.

Maeve, seemingly untouched by the ravages of time, was as beautiful as her daughter. Indeed, a stranger might at first sight have mistaken the two for sisters. Yet, to the seeing eye, Maeve's beauty had with the years acquired a subtle elegance and distinction which little Morag's, for all her youthful freshness, still lacked. But Fraoch, for his part, whether from a due sense of the proprieties, or simply because he lacked discrimination, or perhaps because he was flattered by the poems she kept writing about him, celebrating his beauty, his strength, and his courage, had eyes only for Morag.

As often as he could, Fraoch came to Corul's castle on the shores of Loch Awe, there to pay his court to lovely Morag, to carouse with Corul of the Generous Cups, and, needless to say, to make himself as agreeable as he could to Maeve, his future mother-in-law.

Maeve did nothing to discourage this. When Fraoch rode up to the great gate of the castle, it was she who was there to greet him. After he had spent an hour or so carousing with Corul, it was Maeve who suggested that perhaps by now he had had all he wanted to drink and might care to join her for a quiet talk in her private apartments or for a stroll by the bonny banks of Loch Awe. Meanwhile Morag would be despatched on some tedious but necessary domestic errand.

Fraoch, who for all his good looks, warlike deeds, and kissable lips, had had but little experience of women, fell in readily with Maeve's suggestions and in the end found that he was spending more time with his future mother-in-law than with his betrothed. This, he told himself, was as it should be. He was, after all, going to go through life with little Morag. It was only right that at this stage he should devote as much time as he could to getting to know her mother.

The months went by and one warm summer evening, as Fraoch and Maeve were sitting together in her private apartment while Corul and his boon companions drank themselves into a stupor in the great hall of the castle and Morag busied herself in the stone-flagged kitchen with the preparations for the next great banquet, Maeve moved a little closer than usual to Fraoch and he suddenly found that, without a word passing between them, her hand was in his while her head rested on his shoulder. "If you only knew," she murmured languorously, "how I loved you."

The tone in which this was said and the long lingering kiss which followed her words bewildered Fraoch. He wanted, it is true, to be on the best of terms with his mother-in-law, but this was not quite how he had envisaged their relationship. Disentangling himself as best he could from her embrace, he rose rather awkwardly to his feet. "Perhaps," he said, "I should go and look for Morag. She may be wondering where I am. After all," he went on, with a faint feeling that this was somehow not what was expected of him, "you're still quite pretty. She might even be jealous of you." And he laughed.

Had he but noticed it, even Fraoch might have been alarmed by the look of utter fury which showed for a moment in Maeve's eyes. Coming from him, the words, "you're still quite pretty", had cut her to the quick. And the merry laugh with which he had uttered them was the last straw. What now disgusted her most was the thought that she had ever even considered throwing herself away on this oaf. While showing no overt sign of this sudden change in her feelings towards him, it became her chief purpose in life to destroy Fraoch.

On an island in Loch Awe, says the Seanachie, there was a rowan tree whose fruit was sweeter than honey and could restore youth to the aged and satisfy hunger for the space of three days at a time. But coiled around the tree was a dreadful dragon, most of the time seemingly asleep, with its gaping gorge resting against the trunk of the tree.

Maeve now feigned sickness. She withdrew to her chamber, took to her bed, refused all food, and quickly acquired an interesting pallor which still further enhanced her loveliness. Then, after three or four days, she sent for Fraoch. Confronted with this spectacle of beauty in distress, he rather clumsily expressed his concern, shifting his weight uneasily from one foot to the other as he did so.

"You alone," whispered Maeve from the pile of pillows that supported her, "you alone can save me. If you can bring me just a handful of rowan berries from the tree on the island, I shall be saved. If not, I must die." And she sank back in the bed, looking frailer and more alluring than ever.

For Fraoch, picking fruit was a menial occupation, unworthy of a famous hero. "Fruit have I never stooped to gather," he replied. "But," and he paused, "I will do it for your sake." And that very night, choosing a moment when the dragon appeared to be asleep, he swam silently across to the island, and stepping cautiously over the monster's coils gathered and brought back with him a generous handful of the magic rowan berries.

This was not what Maeve had intended should happen. "That is good," she said, picking at the rowan berries, "very good. But—"

43

and she looked frailer than ever, "—unless you and you alone now bring me the whole rowan tree, torn up by the roots, I die."

However somnolent the dragon might be, uprooting the tree on which it was accustomed to rest its head was bound to waken it, and, once aroused, there could be no telling what it might not do. But Fraoch, as a famous hero, had never recoiled from danger. It was the breath of life to him, his stock in trade. And so, confidently facing what he knew was almost certain death, he once more made his way down to the shore, and, plunging into the icy waters of the loch, again swam vigorously across to the island.

As usual, the dragon was asleep, and Fraoch had torn up the tree by its roots and was already on his way back to the shore before it woke to what was happening. Once awake, however, it moved fast. There was a fearful splash, sending out waves in every direction, and a moment later Fraoch saw the dragon coming after him and, worse still, gaining on him fast.

Although a famous hero, Fraoch was on this occasion unarmed, having left behind his cumbersome spear and shield. His situation seemed desperate. It was now that little Morag, "fairest of form, whitest of hand and warmest of heart", came to the rescue. Running rapidly down to the shore, she handed to her betrothed a sharp knife of gold, which he promptly plunged into the dragon with such good effect that the seething waters of the loch turned red from its blood. But though by now in its death throes, the monster still managed to catch Fraoch bodily in its enormous jaws, and with one last dying bite crushed the life out of him.

"Fraoch," says the Seanachie, "killed the dragon, and the dragon killed Fraoch, and the two fell dead together on the shore of bare stones to the west. The maiden of the fairest form fell down in a swoon. When she awoke, she wailed his lament, and then, sinking down on the bosom of her lover, she too expired. A cairn was raised over the graves of the two lovers on the shore, and the cairn is known as Fraoch's Cairn and the island the Isle of Fraoch or Eilean Fraoch."

What became of the lovely but guileful Maeve who had caused all this havoc, or how she fared thereafter, the Seanachie does not relate. But there are those who to this day, when they speak of Loch Awe, call it by its ancient name of Loch Maeve. So she too need not be entirely forgotten.

A Sister's Curse

TWO ORPHAN SISTERS once lived together in a house on the south side of the beautiful Isle of Mull, one called Lovely Margaret, the other Dun-coloured Ailsa. Lovely Margaret had a slender body, a skin of translucent whiteness, black hair, and enormous blue eyes. Ailsa, to say the least of it, was plain.

To Lovely Margaret there came suddenly one day, when she happened to be alone in the house, a stranger, who was tall, handsome, and fair-haired, with eyes as blue as her own. He told her that he was hungry and thirsty and far from home, and asked if she could spare him something to eat and drink. Liking the look of him, Margaret asked him to come in and sit down, and set before him a jug of milk, a dish of oatcakes and some honey to go with them. These he ate gratefully, and then, taking both her hands in his, he told her that she was as beautiful as she was kind.

Though well aware that she was beautiful, Margaret, like most pretty women, enjoyed being reminded of it, especially by such a handsome man. And so, when he had finished what was on his plate, she went to fetch some more, returning immediately with another dish of oatcakes and honey. But to her surprise, when she came back, she found that the stranger was no longer there. Thinking that perhaps he had gone outside for a moment, she opened the door and looked out. But look where she might, she could see no sign of him, though the house stood on some high ground with a clear view for miles around. As she put away the honey, and the oatcakes, and the jug of milk, she felt displeased and, although she would not have admitted it, a little disappointed. To leave so suddenly after partaking of her hospitality was, she told herself, churlish and ill mannered. Yet, despite his

47

behaviour, she could not deny that she would have liked to see more of her visitor, who was somehow different from any of the men in the neighbouring township, indeed from any man she had ever met.

Next day, Ailsa, to whom Lovely Margaret had said nothing of her encounter, went to visit their aged aunt on the other side of the island, and Margaret was again left alone. As she busied herself about the house, her thoughts turned once more to her visitor of the day before. She would, she had to admit, have liked to see him again, but of that there seemed to be little chance. Feeling tired and dispirited, she had sat down for a moment at the table in the middle of the room when something made her look up and there, standing in the doorway, was the tall, fair-haired stranger.

To her astonishment, her feelings on catching sight of him were of pure delight. Any irritation she might have felt at his sudden departure of the day before or surprise at his equally sudden re-appearance, gave way to sheer pleasure at the thought that he was now once more there with her in the room. Nor, rising to greet him, did she make any attempt to resist him when he took her in his arms and kissed her longingly on the lips. It was, she reflected, in so far as she had any time for reflection, as though he had cast a spell on her. And the same comforting thought again went through her mind next morning, when she looked back in amazement on all that had followed that first passionate embrace.

The next few weeks were for Lovely Margaret a period of utter bliss. Her sister, as it happened, now spent much of her time away from home, so Margaret's lover was free to come and go as he liked. When she least expected him, when he had left her only an hour or two before, he was again suddenly there, as passionate, as totally absorbing as ever. To her he seemed to materialize out of nothing and to vanish again as abruptly into thin air. Nor was it simply the manner of his coming and going that convinced her that this was no ordinary human but rather a stranger from some other world, from the *Sith*, perhaps, from Fairyland. The Gaelic tongue he used was unlike that spoken on Mull or indeed on the mainland, and his whole demeanour was different from that of ordinary men. Even at the height of their love-making there was about him a remoteness that both unnerved her and at the same time bound her more irresistibly to him. Soon his secret visits became for her the only thing that mattered in life.

Her love, meanwhile, had given her a new beauty, a kind of radiance which no one who met her could fail to notice. But to her neighbours' compliments and curiosity she remained impervious, remarking only that fresh air and good food gave any girl a healthy glow. For her lover had made one thing entirely clear. If she ever so much as breathed a word of his visits to anyone, he would vanish from her life as suddenly as he had come into it and never, in any circumstances, reveal himself to her again.

After some months, Dun-coloured Ailsa came back from a more than usually prolonged visit to her aunt with the surprising news that she had found a suitor, Duncan, a worthy man from the other side of the island, who had a dozen cows, some sheep, and a few acres of decent arable land, which produced some of the best corn and hay on the island. They had, said Ailsa, agreed to marry and had already appointed a date for their wedding.

Lovely Margaret was pleased at the news. She would certainly not miss Ailsa's company when she left home to marry, but she was fond of her and wished her well with a husband who sounded ideally suited to her. Although primarily concerned with the affairs of her own heart, she found, rather to her satisfaction, that she could still spare a little affection for her sister. While doubting whether any feeling Ailsa might have for her crofter could properly be dignified by the name of love, she nevertheless talked of it as that. It was love, she told Ailsa at some length, that made the world go round. And Ailsa, wondering what had got into her, listened with surprise to what her sister had to say. There was, said Margaret, warming to her subject, nothing like love. But what, enquired Ailsa, who was nothing if not blunt and who, after their aunt had been put to bed, had already spent a number of happy evenings with her suitor amid his new-mown hay, could Lovely Margaret know of love, to speak of it with such enthusiasm?

Put so directly, the question caught Margaret unawares. Could it really be that she was being asked by her lump of a sister in almost pitying tones what she, Lovely Margaret, knew of love? It was more than she could bear. Very well. She would tell her! She would make Ailsa understand, if understand she could, just what she, Margaret, knew of love. Once she had started, the words came tumbling out, one intimate revelation following another, while Dreary Ailsa sat rooted to her stool.

It was not until half an hour later, when the flood of words finally dried up, that Margaret realized what she had done. She had done what her lover had forbidden her to do. She had told another human being of their secret love. She had put her happiness in peril.

At once she sought to save the situation. "And now, sister," she said, "you will be telling no one."

"No," her sister answered, "I will not be telling anyone; that story will as soon pass from my lips as it will from my knee." And Margaret went away, at any rate partly reassured.

But Ailsa was only human. She had not in her dull life had many secrets to keep, and to keep this one was more than she was capable of. That very night, sitting by the fire, in the strictest confidence she told her suitor's mother of Margaret's mysterious lover: of how he was suddenly there and no less suddenly away; of how he made love more passionately and more potently than any man on earth: of how, in a word, he seemed to hold Lovely Margaret in thrall.

Listening avidly to Ailsa's words, the old body nodded sagely.

She had, she said, heard of such things before, many, many years ago. Of one thing they could be sure: Margaret's lover was no ordinary mortal. He came, without doubt, from the *Sith*, from Fairyland, and would in due course return there. And to Margaret and her kin he would bring nothing but sorrow. Nothing, she repeated in a high, dismal wail, but sorrow. Nothing but sorrow.

Belatedly, Ailsa understood that she had betrayed her sister's confidence. Clearly, no force on earth would stop her future mother-in-law from telling her tale, with embellishments, to all the other old wives in the township. Full of remorse, she urged the old woman to secrecy, but in her own mind she already knew it would be of no avail.

A week went by and Margaret, now alone in the house, continued to look forward to her lover's next visit. As far as she was concerned there was nothing else to look forward to, nothing else to live for. All she thought of were ways to please him, ways of making him happier and more comfortable when he next came, ways of making herself more acceptable to him. With this in mind, she busied herself about the house and looked at herself critically in the mirror. With this in mind, she lay down each night in her lonely bed, half hoping that she would wake up, as she had woken more than once, to find him suddenly there beside her. But this did not happen, and when on some errand she walked down to the township it seemed to her that the women in the street looked at her askance, while the men, too, now looked at her differently from before.

Another week went by, and a third, and still her lover did not return. On her next visit to the township, the knowing looks which followed her left her in no doubt that her secret was out. In no doubt, either, that her lover, if he sought to visit her, would learn this too. Margaret was distraught. The thought of his cold rage filled her with fear, but that she was ready to face. Ready, indeed, for anything save the danger that he might be as good as his word and simply never come back. Ready for anything rather than the inescapable truth which now at length began to stare her in the face: namely, that she would never see him again as long as she lived.

"And," says the Seanachie, taking up the story at this point, "when he came again, he found that he was observed, and he went away and never returned, nor was he seen or heard of ever after by anyone. And when the lovely sister came to know this, she left her home and became a wanderer among the hills and hollows, and never afterwards came inside a house door to stand or sit down while she lived. Those who herded cattle tried frequently to get near her, but they never succeeded further than to hear her crooning a melancholy song in which she told how her sister had been false to her and how, if the fairies had any power, the wrong done would in time be avenged on her sister or her descendants...." And on her sister and her kin they heard her utter this curse:

"May nothing on which you have set your expectations ever grow,
Nor dew ever fall on your ground.
May no smoke rise from your dwelling.
In the depths of the hardest winter,
May the worm be in your store,
And the moth under the lid of your chests.
If a fey being has power,
Revenge will be taken, though it may be on your descendants."

Not long after these disturbing events, Ailsa celebrated her marriage to Duncan, and in due course a son was born to them, Torquil, who in time grew up to be a sturdy brown-haired youth, better looking than either his mother or his father and famous throughout the island as a reaper. Indeed, it was said that he could reap as much as seven other men and that none could get the better of him.

One night, when Torquil had finished reaping, some friends told him that a strange, beautiful woman had been seen that autumn in the harvest fields. She would come to the fields, they said, in the evening, after the reapers had left, and would alone reap a whole field before daylight next morning. They called her *Gruagach a' Chuirn*, the Maiden of the Cairn, because to those who had seen her she seemed to come out of a pile of stones on the hillside.

This tale aroused Torquil's curiosity and also his pride as a reaper, and he resolved to wait in the fields one evening in the hope that he might catch a glimpse of the Maiden at work. And so it happened that one Sunday night, when he had been working later than usual, Torquil, chancing to look back as he was making his way home, saw her starting work in the field he had just left. Although with a wild look in her eye, she was astonishingly lovely and, from the way in which she wielded the sickle, seemed possessed of supernatural energy. Determined to overtake her, Torquil picked up his sickle and went after her. But the harder he reaped, the greater the distance grew between them. *"Ghruagach a' Chuirn"*, he cried, *"fuirich rium, fuirich rium"* "Maiden of the Cairn, wait for me, wait for me!"

"Handsome, brown-haired youth," came her reply, "overtake me, overtake me!"

More determined than ever to overtake her, Torquil worked on until a cloud covered the moon. "The moon is darkened by a cloud," he called out. "Delay, delay!"

"The moon is my only light," she answered enigmatically. "Overtake me, overtake me!"

But try as he would, Torquil could not overtake her, and seeing how far ahead of him she now was, he called out despairingly, "I am weary with reaping. Wait for me, wait for me." But from high above him on the hillside, again came her eerie cry, "Overtake me, overtake me!"

In the end, as Torquil struggled after her, the Maiden reached the head of the last furrow and stood there waiting for him in the moonlight, sickle in hand, beautiful and yet somehow menacing.

In those days there was a tradition in the Highlands and Islands whereby the reaper would take home with him the last handful of corn, to cut and fashion into a doll, known as the Harvest Maiden, which he would keep until the following year. This was done on any day save only Monday, the Day of the Moon, when to make such a doll betokened disaster. So now, when Torquil came to the head of his last furrow, he caught up the last handful of corn and, not realizing that it was by now past midnight on Sunday, stood before the Maiden and faced her with the doll in one hand and his sickle in the other. But she, looking

53

down on him, simply said. *"S dona an ni moch Di-luain dol a bhuain maighdein,"* "It is an evil thing to reap the Harvest Maiden early on a Monday." "Whereupon" says the Seanachie, "Torquil fell dead in the field and never more drew breath. As for the Maiden of the Cairn, she was never afterwards seen; and that was how the sister's wish was fulfilled."

Princess Thyra

MANY CENTURIES AGO a son of the King of Denmark came to Loch Maree in Wester Ross to hunt deer and, while out on the hill one day, became separated from his companions. Feeling tired, he sat down by the side of the path and fell asleep. On waking, he heard the sound of voices and saw two men and a young girl approaching. "He got up," says the Seanachie, "and as they were coming nearer he was making out that he never saw a more beautiful woman." Standing in the middle of the path, he accosted the three and, when the older of the two men called on him to get out of their way, rebuked him for his insolence, pointing out that he was a prince, with the blood of the Danish kings in his veins.

At this the old man excused himself. They had come, he said, from the nearby monastery of Islemaree, situated on an island in the loch, and must return thither before nightfall. It was his especial duty to protect the young girl they had with them, who, by her father's command, was under the vows of the church.

"I would like well to know," enquired the young prince, "who this maiden is you have with you."

"Her name," replied the old man, "is Princess Thyra of the mighty royal house of Ulster in Erin. And now let us pass." As they went their respective ways, the prince said sadly to the maiden, "This was our first meeting. I fear it may be our last. Farewell."

"I would not say *that*," replied Princess Thyra promptly, giving him a charming smile.

Thus encouraged, the prince returned more than once to Loch Maree in the hope of again meeting the princess and, when

disappointed in this, hired a boat to take him across to the island.
On reaching the monastery, he asked for the princess, saying
that he would like to make her his wife. In due course Princess
Thyra appeared and made him welcome, and the two spent the
day together on the island. But, before the prince left again, the
princess, who was not entirely inexperienced in such things, said
to him, "I have a doubt in this matter."

"What is that?" he asked.

"It is," she replied "that I never saw you but once before.
Neither did you see me. If love came quickly, it may go as
quickly."

"Do you know that from yourself?" the prince asked.

"No," she said.

Whereupon, pointing to the evening star in the southwestern
sky, "As truly as that star shines on yonder hill," the prince
declared, "so truly do I love you."

"I have another doubt," she said.

"Your doubts are many," he replied.

"There is," she went on, "in this region a man they call Red
Hector of the Hills, a big, strong man, who is in the hills day and
night and who would kill you as soon as look at you. I fear that,
were you to encounter him, you would find him a dangerous

enemy." But the prince laughed at the idea that this should worry him, and left Islemaree with the feeling that things were going well for him.

Making his way back to the mainland the prince now set out to rejoin his companions, humming a merry tune as he went. He had not gone far when an arrow whistled past his head, and a second lodged in his bonnet. Looking up, he saw ahead of him a big burly red-haired man with a beard standing beside a rock by the roadside.

"Who are you, and why do you use me as a target?" asked the prince.

"And have you never heard," enquired the other, "of *Eachann Ruadh nan Cnoc,* Red Hector of the Hills? If not, you see him before you now. Moreover, you will soon experience his skill as a swordsman, for I can assure you there is a matter between us which can only be settled in one of two ways. Either you kill me, or I kill you." At which each drew his sword, and they set to with a will. Before very long the prince received a severe wound, and Red Hector made off, leaving him for dead.

Next day, some people from the island, finding the unfortunate prince lying there senseless, took him to the monastery, where, with the help of Princess Thyra, he was nursed slowly back to health.

The more he and Thyra saw of each other, the stronger their attachment became, and, says the Seanachie, the prince told her every day how he would take her to Denmark.

Then one day a boat arrived at Loch Maree from Ireland, bringing the sad news that Thyra's father lay close to death and that she must go back to Ulster.

"Will you return?" asked the prince.

"I will return," replied Thyra.

"And will you forget me among your own people?" asked the prince.

"Nothing but death will prevent my return," she said.

At about this time, the prince, while on a visit to the mainland, encountered a big, burly man with reddish hair, no longer in his first youth, whose appearance seemed somehow familiar to him. His name, the man announced, was Dougal Mackenzie, and he entreated the prince to take him into his service and give him shelter. The prince was at first reluctant to employ him. "Have you no house or home?" he asked.

"I had one yesterday," Dougal replied sadly. "Today, I have nothing. I had house, wife, son, land, cattle. And yesterday every beast I had was lifted save one stray sheep, and my son went in search of it and fell over the rocks and was killed. And when his mother heard what had happened to him, she went to the place, and on seeing her son dead she leapt into the sea and was drowned, and I am left alone. If you will take me, I will serve you better on the hill than a younger man ever would." And the prince, listening to this sad story, took pity on him and agreed to employ him for as long as he remained in Wester Ross awaiting Thyra's return.

For months nothing was heard of Princess Thyra, and in his impatience the prince sent men each day to the top of the highest hill to watch for the return of her ship. Finally, one day they saw three ships approaching, the largest flying the royal standard of Ulster at the topmast. Excited, the prince immediately started for the top of the nearest hill, but Dougal Mackenzie, who happened to be with him, sought to hold him back. "Wait," he said, "till I tell you my dream."

"I care nothing for dreams," said the prince.

"Will you not listen?" said Dougal, "for I dreamt the same dream three nights running. And it was that she was dead."

"I was hoping for joyful news," rejoined the prince, "and you bring me ill tidings."

"I have an idea," said Dougal, still seeking to delay him. "Let me do this: I will go out to the ship, and if all is well you will see a red signal. But if sorrow awaits you, it will be a black one."

Having finally obtained his master's agreement, Dougal went out to the ship and there found Thyra safe and sound. When she saw him, her first question was whether all was well with the prince and if he was not impatient for news of her. After reassuring her, Dougal now put forward a complicated plan of his own, which, he said, would cause the prince the most joy of all. First, Thyra would show the death signal, then, when she landed and her lover saw that she was in fact alive, he would, said Dougal, be even happier than if she had hoisted the red signal in the first place. With some misgivings, Thyra agreed. The black signal was displayed and the royal standard flown at half mast. But the result was by no means as happy as Dougal had said it would be. When the prince saw the death signal hoisted, he cried out that he now had no further wish to live and, drawing his dirk, killed himself.

And so, when Thyra herself landed not long after, those who met her had to tell her that her lover, believing her to be dead, had taken his own life. On hearing this, she at once asked to be taken to where he lay, and, on being shown his body, turned angrily on Dougal. "Wretched Dougal!" she said. "What evil advice you gave me!"

This was the moment Dougal had been waiting for. "Dougal is not my name," he replied, drawing himself up to his full height and snatching off his bonnet to reveal his grizzled red locks. "I am Red Hector of the Hills," he cried, "and this," plunging his dirk into her, "is my revenge!" For, as Thyra herself had perhaps more than half suspected, he, in his own way, had loved her too.

The Norse King's Daughter

LONG AGO, in the days of the Norse invasions of the Western Highlands, the Norse invaders were dismayed by the quality and extent of the pine forest which then covered the greater part of Lochaber and which in every respect surpassed the forests of their native land.

At that time the Norse King had a daughter who, besides being dazzlingly beautiful, with her long fair hair and blue eyes and slender, pliant body, was known far and wide for her many skills and not least for her proficiency in the black arts. The flowers of the woods and meadows were all well known to her, and there was not a herb with whose properties she was not acquainted. She was likewise famed for her skill with cattle, being able to undo any spell or charm that was laid on them and to cure them of any sickness or injury that befell them. To her, the lowing of cattle was the sweetest of all sounds, and she would answer it herself across great distances. But of all her skills the most unusual, and one of the most useful, was her ability, when necessary, to fly through the air high above the countryside so that no obstacle could hinder her progress.

Having a high opinion of his daughter's gifts, the Norse King often consulted her when his other advisers failed him, and it was to her that he now turned in his search for a means of destroying the woodlands of Lochaber, which offered such dangerous competition to his own country's forests.

Apprised of the problem, the lovely princess, always glad to oblige her aged parent, had no doubt at all what to do. Setting fire to the selvage of her dress, she soared high over the North Sea and swooped down on Lochaber. "And," says the Seanachie, "the sparks of fire that flew from her dress were blown hither and thither by the wind, and the woods set on fire, until the whole countryside was in a haze and so darkened by smoke that it was impossible to see... And the people gathered to watch her, but from the swiftness of her descent they could not grasp her and were at a loss what to do. And at last they sought instruction from a learned man in the place, who advised them to collect a herd of cattle in a field and, when she heard the lowing of the cattle, she would descend, and when she was within gunshot they were to fire at her with a silver bullet, when she would become a faggot of bones.

"This advice they followed and began to gather cattle and follow after her. And when she heard the cry of the herd she descended, and they aimed at her with a silver bullet, as the wise man had told them to do, and she fell gently among them. After this, men lifted her remains and carried them to Lochaber, and to make sure that, dead or alive, she would do no more injury to them, they buried her in Achnacarry. And no more than a hundred years ago, the teller of this tale claimed that he could put his foot on the place where she lay buried."

When news of his daughter's death reached the Norse King, he sent a ship to bring her back, but by their incantations the Lochaber women, who were likewise skilled in witchcraft, destroyed it: the boat was wrecked, and the men lost at the entrance to Locheil. Nor did the next ship he sent fare better. And so the third time the King sent his whole fleet. But when his ships were seen approaching, the people of the island of Iona raised a storm by emptying the wells on the Fairy Hill, which made the wind blow in whatever direction they chose. "And the storm," says the Seanachie, "was so violent and the ships so near that the entire fleet was driven on the shore beneath the Fairy Hill, and the power and might of the Norsemen was broken and so much weakened that they did not return again to infest the land."

Caivala of the Glossy Hair

IN THE DAYS of Donald, Second Lord of the Isles, Donald's younger brother, Iain Mor MacDonald of Kintyre, went to Erin to hunt. One day, while out hunting, he met in a narrow glen a big, rascally looking fellow with curly black hair, riding a horse, with a lovely glossy-haired maiden up behind him, who, for her part, was weeping and loudly bewailing her fate. The man, whose name was O'Docherty, had, it seemed, carried off the maiden after a fight with her father, whom he had left bleeding in the heather nearby. With a scowl, O'Docherty told Mac-Donald to get out of his way. Iain Mor replied that he would not do so until he knew why the maiden was weeping so bitterly. At this, O'Docherty, who was powerfully built, got down from his horse in a rage, and, drawing his sword, set about MacDonald with a will. MacDonald fought back and, although severely wounded, in the end prevailed.

Leaving O'Docherty for dead, MacDonald went with the maiden, whose name, it appeared, was Caivala of the Glossy Hair, to the place where her father, who, she said, was the most noble Earl of Antrim, lay bleeding in the heather. Together they carried her father back to his castle, where Iain Mor remained until his wounds had healed. While he was there, he and Caivala of the Glossy Hair spent much time singing songs and ballads together, their voices blending in happy harmony.

When Iain Mor was fit to travel, he asked leave to speak to Caivala's father in private, and on being admitted to his presence, announced that he wished to marry his lovely daughter. To this, Antrim, who, like many others, traced his ancestry back to the High Kings of Ireland, replied that he regarded Iain Mor's request as insulting and presumptuous in the extreme.

"I," retorted Iain Mor, "am Lord of Kintyre and full brother to the Lord of the Isles and King of the Hebrides. If lovely Caivala of the Glossy Hair were to become my wife, there could be peace and friendship between us for ever." At which, Antrim, who did not fully appreciate the exalted position occupied in Western Scotland by the Lords of the Isles and their kin, grew angrier than ever, and, summoning some men at arms, had the unfortunate youth consigned to a dark, dismal dungeon with heavy

gates of brass and locks of iron and no more than a single bottle of straw to lie on.

That very night, as he lay amid the straw, Iain Mor was suddenly woken by the sound of the great iron locks and heavy brass gates being opened. This, he thought, must be his jailer coming to finish him off. Seizing a great iron sledgehammer which someone had left lying there, he at once leapt to his feet and assumed a defensive posture. But a pleasant surprise awaited him.

"Fear nothing, it is I," said lovely Caivala, opening the heavy brass gates. "I have stolen the keys from under my father's head as he slept and a swift *birlinn* galley now waits below, ready to carry you across the sea." And not many hours later Iain Mor was safely back in Kintyre.

The Earl of Antrim, who had no son, now sought to prevail on his daughter to marry any one of several handpicked suitors of noble birth and great possessions, for he greatly desired an heir. But Caivala stubbornly rejected them all, repeating that the only man she would ever marry was Iain Mor MacDonald from Kintyre across the sea. "Enraged by her obstinacy," says the Seanachie, "her father now built a castle on a cliff high above the ocean, where no vessel could come near that the men in the castle could not sink by throwing stones at it. In this she was immured with a guard on her."

On learning where Caivala was confined, Iain Mor decided to go over to Erin in the hope of catching even a glimpse of her. Leaving Kintyre one evening in his swift *birlinn,* he reached Antrim early next morning. As he approached the castle in which Caivala was imprisoned, he could hear her singing one of the songs which in happier times they had sung together. In a low but melodious voice, he joined in the chorus, whereupon she looked out of the window and, to her delight, saw her lover standing on the ship's deck below. Snatching the sheets from her bed and knotting them together to form a rope, she promptly let it down to him. With its help, he clambered nimbly up to her, and, after carefully lowering her to safety, followed himself. By good fortune, her guards, being asleep, never noticed her departure. Together, Caivala and Iain Mor now sailed for Kintyre, arriving that very night on the sandy shore of *Machaire Mor na*

Moralachd, or Noble Macharimore, where they were welcomed with enthusiasm and due ceremony by Iain Mor's loyal clansmen.

Not long after this, Iain Mor received a menacing message from the Earl of Antrim to say that, unless he sent his daughter back at once, it would be the worse for him. To this MacDonald replied that if Antrim wanted a fight he could have one, but he would probably get more than he bargained for. If, however, he was prepared for peace, this might in the long run be better for all concerned.

Seeing that MacDonald was quite determined to keep Caivala of the Glossy Hair, Antrim now had second thoughts and invited the lovers to come and visit him in his great castle, where he received them most hospitably. After which, he and MacDonald swore eternal friendship.

The years went by, and on Antrim's death Iain Mor succeeded him as earl, with the happy result that the MacDonalds, or as it is now written, MacDonnells, have been Earls of Antrim ever since and are to this day still proud of their longstanding family connection with the most noble Lords of the Isles and Kings of the Hebrides.

*   *   *   *

In fact, the records show that Iain Mor MacDonald of Kintyre, younger brother of Donald of the Isles, married Mary or Marjory, the heiress of John Bisset, Lord of the Glens of Antrim. Iain Mor was later (before 1427) murdered by a man called James Campbell, sent to kill him by King James I. "But," says the chronicler, "because Campbell had no written order to produce in his defence, he was taken and beheaded, *which shows the dangerous consequences of undertaking such a service without due circumspection.*" Ian Mor's descendant, Sir Randal MacSorley MacDonnell, son of the notorious Sorley Buie or Sorley Boy, was created first Earl of Antrim by James VI in 1620.

The Isles of the Sea

SAILING SOUTHWARDS from the Isle of Mull down the Sound of Lorne on a clear day, the first thing that catches your eye are four craggy islands with a scattering of small rocks around them — the half-submerged peaks, one could imagine, of some primeval mountain range. These are the Isles of the Sea, a retreat many centuries ago for the holy men who first brought Christianity to the West of Scotland. On the southernmost island, *Eileach an Naoimh,* the Isle of the Saint, are still to be seen the ruined chapel and beehive cells of a monastery founded in 542 by Saint Brendan of Clonfert, and later dwelt in by Saint Columba himself, whose mother, Eithne, they say, lies buried there. By some, *Eileach an Naoimh* is thought to be the fabled Hinba, where Columba prayed with such intensity that a sacred radiance shone forth from his cell.

In contrast to its neighbours, *Dun Chonnuill* or Dunconnel, the northernmost of the islands, was of strategic rather than religious importance. On it, commanding the Sound of Lorne, stood the stronghold of Conal, King of Dalriada, which was to pass, much later, into the possession of his remote descendants, the MacDonald Lords of the Isles and Kings of the Hebrides. During their tenure, in the second half of the fourteenth century, Dunconnel was the scene of what the historian William Forbes Skene has called "one of the most daring actions ever recorded of any Highland chief".

Among those who frequented the court of John MacDonald of the Isles at his great castle of Ardtornish on the Sound of Mull, there were few livelier characters than Lachlan and Hector, the sons of MacDonald's close kinsman, *Iain Dubh* or Black John,

Third Chief of Clan Maclean. Like their father, Iain Dubh, and their grandfather, Gille-Caluim, who had fought with Bruce at Bannockburn, both were outstanding warriors. The elder of the two, *Lachlan Lubanach* or Lachlan the Wily, was, as his name suggests, a master of manoeuvre and dissimulation, a resourceful tactician and diversionary, and, when necessary, a skilled negotiator. He also took care to be the best-informed man in the Western Highlands, quickly becoming a veritable repository of useful political, social, and military intelligence. His younger brother, *Eachann Reaganach* or Hector the Ferocious, was a man of rather different character and capabilities. After Lachlan had planned a military or paramilitary operation and completed the preliminary manoeuvring, Hector, a heavyweight in every sense of the word, would come in for the kill, manfully swinging his family's ancestral battle-axe, which the founder and name-father of the clan, *Gilleoin na Tuaighe* or Gillean of the Battle Axe, had wielded to such excellent effect against the Norwegians at the Battle of Largs a century before.

Socially, this formidable pair revealed a different side to their characters. However wily, Lachlan was clever enough not to let this appear in society, while Hector, although quite exceptionally ferocious in battle, displayed when off duty a number of the most endearing characteristics. In the words of the Seanachie, "the prominence of their father and their own affable and pleasing manners soon gained for them the friendship of John, first Lord of the Isles".

To a young man of ambition, the friendship of Good John, as he was popularly known, was an invaluable asset. As Lord of the Isles and King of the Hebrides, he was, in theory at any rate, the man who counted in the Western Highlands, the monarch, for most practical purposes, of all he surveyed. And then there was something else. Of all the fair maidens who graced Good John's court, none was lovelier than his own daughter Mairi. With her black hair, clear, ivory-coloured skin, high cheekbones, generous mouth, slightly upturned nose, lissom body, and, last but not least, limpid blue eyes, frequently compared by the bards at her father's court to twin pools of light, Mairi was a true West Highland beauty. What is more, in marked contrast to most of her silly little companions, Mairi was as clever (some would have said as devious) as she was beautiful, a characteristic which appealed strongly to quick-witted Lachlan, who, it may be observed, could not bear stupid women, although to further his career he might at a pinch have put up with one.

The attraction was mutual. At court the opportunities for philandering were limited, but Lachlan and Mairi were ingenious enough to take the fullest advantage of them. Soon a secret attachment sprang up between the pair.

"What do you think Father will say if he finds out?" asked Mairi.

"Leave that to me," repled Wily Lachlan with yet another long, lingering look.

As the acknowledged friend and kinsman of the Lord of the Isles and his daughter's secret lover, Lachlan Lubanach's position at court was a strong one, while Fierce Hector's affable manners soon made him a host of friends. But popular as both brothers were, it is never easy to be friends with everyone. The greater and more obvious Good John's liking for the

brothers became, the more his Master of the Household, Niall Mac-Gillebride Mackinnon, Chief of Clan Mackinnon, came to detest them and the more determined he became to get rid of them. Not only was he jealous of the two brothers, he literally could not endure the sight of them, missing no opportunity to insult them in public and even jeering at the rough and ready way in which they ate their food. In his determination to do away with them, Mackinnon enjoyed the enthusiastic support of his brother Fingon, the Mitred Abbot of Iona, "a subtle and wicked councillor", says the Seanachie, who in his vulpine way hated not only the Macleans, but, it was rumoured, the very Lords of the Isles themselves.

Like the Macleans, the Mackinnons, who at that time held sway over large areas of Mull, were of the kindred of Saint Columba and, like them, for this reason carried a hand bearing a cross on their coat of arms. As a clan this gave them considerable standing in local ecclesiastical circles. But far away in Rome, His Holiness the Pope had serious reservations about them and had long refused to recognize Fingon Mackinnon, popularly known as the Green Abbot, as Abbot of Iona. For one thing, Fingon had fathered several children by the lady of his choice, a practice which, although more or less acceptable to the old Celtic Church, was viewed with disfavour by Rome. For another, Fingon had shown himself actively hostile to the monks of the Benedictine order who had been sent to Iona at His Holiness's direct behest. Indeed, there had been savage clashes between opposing sects, the native clergy seeking to drive out the incomers by force of arms. None of which, needless to say, prevented that "subtle and wicked councillor", the Green Abbot, from continuing to play an active and usually mischievous part in local affairs.

The occasion which Niall MacGillebride Mackinnon picked to rid himself of Lachlan and Hector was a great tinchal, or deer hunt, on the Isle of Mull, to which Good John had, as a sign of his especial favour, bidden both brothers. Mackinnon's plan was a simple one: at the right moment two well-aimed arrows would find their marks, not in one or other of the fine stags for which Mull is still famous, but in the very vitals, first, of quick-witted Lachlan and then of his brother Hector. This task Mackinnon assigned to two of his most trusted and experienced bowmen, known alike for their presence of mind and accuracy of aim.

Mackinnon's mistake was to talk about his plan in advance. True, he discussed it only with the two bowmen, with his brother the Abbot, and with the members of his own immediate circle. But, as it happened, one of these was on closer terms than most people realized with quick-witted Lachlan, to whom he was under some kind of an obligation, and in due course the following conversation took place between them.

"Might you, Lachlan Lubanach, be intending to be taking part in the great tinchal which we hear is being held by the Most Exalted Lord of the Isles?"

"It is true that my noble kinsman has been gracious enough to invite my brother and myself and, if the circumstances at the time were to prove propitious, it is possible that I might, as you say, consider taking part."

"Should you, after due consideration, be deciding that you will be taking part, it would, Lachlan Lubanach, be to your advantage to be thinking very carefully just where you might be standing. It is said that two of Niall MacGillebride's best bowmen will be culling two young stags which of late have in one way or another been causing trouble in the herd. Even the best archers might sometimes be happening to hit the wrong target, the more so when what might be called an outside influence is directing their aim."

After which the conversation turned to other topics and before long Lachlan's visitor took his leave.

It would have been unlike either Lachlan or his equally heroic brother Hector to refuse an assignation simply because of any element of danger involved. On the day of the great tinchal, therefore, when the moment came for the deer to be driven in the direction of the carefully aligned marksmen, both were well to the fore. So much to the fore that one was standing on either side of the Lord of the Isles himself. Nor did either leave Good John's side for a moment; indeed, both shot more than one deer intended for Good John. Nor could the most expert marksman have put an arrow into either brother without serious risk of striking down his sovereign liege.

No sooner was the tinchal over than the two brothers made haste to withdraw, first asking Mackinnon with a nasty sneer whether he had enjoyed his day's sport. Of one thing both were now quite certain: Mackinnon must go. Had he not on a previous occasion gone so far as to comment unfavourably on their table manners? And now he was trying to kill them, all without any real provocation on their part.

It was known that soon after his great tinchal the Lord of the Isles would set sail from Mull in his state galley for his castle of Ardtornish on the mainland, leaving Mackinnon as Master of the Household to follow at his leisure in his own lighter and swifter longboat. As usual, well-informed, quick-witted Lachlan saw his opportunity. What he had in mind would be better attended to once Good John was out of the way.

In order to embark, Mackinnon would need to walk the length of the narrow stone jetty at Craignure on the eastern side of the island. At that moment he would present an easy target to a cleverly situated marksman.

A little before sunrise on the appointed day, a reliable Maclean bowman was concealed behind the battlements of a disused watchtower near the jetty, while Lachlan and Hector and a score of their men at arms took up positions just inside the entrance to the tower, ready to rush out as and when the situation demanded it. From their hiding place, they first watched the Lord of the Isles and his attendants go on board his great galley which then set sail immediately. Next, Mackinnon made his appearance, and, after taking leave of a few minor court officials who had come to see him off, started to walk along the jetty towards his longboat.

This was the moment for which the Macleans had been waiting. From his vantage point, the bowman watched Mackinnon's every move. Waiting until his victim was halfway along the jetty with his back turned to the shore, he put a first arrow fair and square between Mackinnon's shoulders and a second into his prostrate carcase, as it lay slumped on the jetty. A moment later Lachlan and Hector and their men at arms had rushed from their hiding place, trampling Mackinnon's body underfoot as they bludgeoned their way on board the waiting longboat. Taken unawares, not many of the dead Chief's retainers put up much resistance, and those who did were quickly despatched with a few swings of Hector's mighty axe. In a matter of minutes the Macleans were not only on board the longboat but in possession of it.

Once the bodies of Mackinnon's dead henchmen had been dropped over the side and any prisoners they had taken duly disposed of, Lachlan and Hector sat down to consider their next move. The first phase of their operation had been successfully completed: Mackinnon had been killed. Where did they go from here?

What they could not be entirely sure of was how the Lord of the Isles would react to the elimination of the Master of his Household. It was true that Good John was their cousin and had of late shown them a high degree of favour. On the other hand, Mackinnon had been a powerful personage at court with many powerful friends and great possessions in Mull and elsewhere. Moreover, his brother Fingon, the subtle and wicked Green Abbot, had also to be reckoned with, not to mention his numerous and no less wicked progeny. It was thus always possible that Good John, although not by nature choleric, might view with displeasure the high-handed manner in which his Master of the Household had been sent to another world and contemplate withdrawing his favour from his sprightly young cousins. He might even, with the very considerable forces at his command, decide to take disciplinary action against them. The dreaded words "fire and sword" crossed their minds. What is more, that accursed Abbot, a born intriguer, might well arrange for their excommunication, not with Rome, where his standing was low, but locally, which, as good churchmen, would in some ways cause them even greater embarrassment. These were eventualities which they must at all costs avoid. How were they to do it?

At that moment the object of their concern was on the high seas, or at any rate somewhere in the Sound of Mull, less than an hour's sailing from where they sat. On board with him were a few court officials and no more than a handful of sailors and men at arms whom they had themselves watched go on board Good John's slow-moving state galley. Indeed, quick-witted Lachlan, always on the lookout for useful information, had actually taken a note of their numbers, fewer, he had observed, than his own little band of brothers. Already a plan was beginning to take shape in his fertile mind. In Mackinnon's streamlined longboat, they could easily outsail and overtake Good John's great galley. The question was: what then?

Just then Ferocious Hector, whose thoughts had been slowly moving in the same direction, suddenly spoke up. In council, as in battle, he had a way of going straight to the point. "We could kill them all," he said.

"Yes," said Lachlan patiently, "but I might be after thinking of a cleverer way." And Hector, who since childhood had recognized his elder brother's superiority of intellect and greater subtlety of thought, kept quiet while he continued. "We could," said Lachlan, "do something else. We could take Good John prisoner and keep him as our prisoner until he agrees to do all we want him to do. And for my part, I can think of a number of things I might be wanting him to do. Once committed to us, the Lord of the Isles and King of the Hebrides would be a valuable ally. Good John is not a difficult man, nor are the few courtiers who are with him today. It is the others at Ardtornish who could be difficult: the commander of the men at arms, and the admiral of his fleet, not to mention that unspeakable Green Abbot. Those are the people we would have against us if we killed Good John — the army, the navy, and the church. And remember, my dear brother, that at this moment they are much, much stronger than we are. But with Good John on our side, not to say in our pocket, there would be no end to what we could do.

"And then," he added in a rather different tone, "there is Mairi...," but did not for the moment pursue this line of thought. Instead, "To your oars," he shouted at the top of his voice. "We can work out a plan as we go."

Barely half an hour later Lachlan's men were in sight of Good John's galley and not long after that were alongside. From the poop, Good John himself watched them with interest as they swarmed up the side. He was, as usual, delighted to see his young cousins, although a little puzzled by the manner of their arrival and rather astonished, too, at the unceremonious way in which their men at arms followed them up the side of the state galley. "I see Mackinnon has lent you his longboat," he said.

"In a manner of speaking, yes" replied Lachlan.

"Will he be following later himself?" asked Good John.

"I think we can say he will not," said Lachlan.

Always an excellent host, Good John felt a dram or two might be a help. "Will you be partaking of a refreshment?" he graciously enquired. A flagon was brought, and John, who meantime had noticed that a Maclean man at arms was now stationed next to the helmsman, while his companions had distributed themselves tactically throughout the ship, poured out three generous measures.

Never at a loss for words, Lachlan broke the ice. "Most noble Prince," he began, feeling that the occasion required a more formal approach than usual, "we have what I fear may be disturbing news for you. Mackinnon, whom you so graciously appointed Master of your Household, on whom you lavished so many other honours and favours; Mackinnon, your supposed friend and ally, was from the first a traitor, a traitor both to Your Majesty and to the Kingdom of the Isles—".

"You say 'was'," interjected Good John.

"I say 'was'," replied Lachlan, "for the simple reason that the villain is no more. With the loyal help of Hector here, I slew him before he could do any more harm to you or, for that matter, to anyone else. And now I am come with all speed to apprise you of the fact and to join Your Majesty in rejoicing at the villain's downfall."

If Good John felt any distress at the news he had just received, he was careful not to show it. Politics, he had come to realize, like others before and since, were the art of the possible. In the circumstances in which he found himself, the only possibility open to him was to listen politely to what was said. The mere sight of Hector Reaganach fingering the razor-sharp blade of his battle-axe made him feel uneasy. Besides, he had to admit that he liked being addressed as "Most Noble Prince" and "Your Majesty". Not enough people did it. He must speak to his Master of the Household about it — when he had one again. After all, he was King of the Hebrides.

Meanwhile there was one point that needed clearing up: namely, the course his galley was now taking. Ardtornish, for which he had been making, was by this time fast vanishing to port. "We seem," he said mildly, for he was essentially a mild man, "to be sailing not in the direction of my castle of Ardtornish but directly away from it. And, if I am not mistaken, one of your men has now taken the helm."

"That," said Lachlan, "is a purely precautionary measure, nothing, I can assure Your Majesty, to be alarmed at. We felt," and here Hector nodded knowingly, "that it would be better if, now that Mackinnon is no more, the three of us had a quiet talk about the future. There are many important decisions of policy to be taken in a number of different fields, which is why we are at this very moment sailing not eastwards to Your Majesty's castle of Ardtornish, but southwards to another of Your Majesty's castles, the fortress of Dunconnel, first built many centuries ago, as you will doubtless recall, by Your Majesty's, and my own, most noble forebear, Conal, King of Dalriada. Not only is it secluded, it has the added advantage of being practically impregnable. A mere handful of men can effectively defend it against an army or, for that matter, a navy. While we remain there we shall be in no danger of interruption — no danger whatever. What is more, in order to prepare this rough fortress for Your Majesty's sojourn there, I have sent my new longboat on ahead with a number of my most dependable men at arms to see to everything."

To Good John, less familiar than he might have been with some of the outposts of his miniature empire, the formidable rock fortress of Dunconnel came as a not altogether pleasant surprise. First of all, it was far from clear to him how they could ever

land on it or, having landed, ever get off it again. To the north, west and south, cliffs of sheer rock dropped perpendicularly to the sea, several hundred feet below, while the island's eastern side was broken by a couple of craggy inlets, neither of which seemed readily navigable. Already the breeze was freshening, and the sea was breaking over the jagged rocks for which they were heading.

But none of this deterred Lachlan's sturdy henchmen for a moment. In a flash, one gigantic man at arms had lifted his sovereign liege over the side of his great galley and down into a tiny coracle, where another was waiting to carry him with a few powerful strokes of his oars through the heavy seas into a narrow creek. There, more strong arms seized hold of him and hoisted him, with perhaps less ceremony than the occasion might have seemed to demand, up a steep flight of rough stone steps and into the castle itself. His last impression, as the great door clanged to behind him, was that the breeze, if you could call it that, was now freshening still further.

The gale which struck the west coast of Scotland that night was long remembered with horror by the inhabitants, but, despite the damage it did, nothing could have been better suited to the purposes of Lachlan Lubanach and his brother Hector. While the wind howled round the castle keep and great seas broke over the rocks below, no power on earth, save the waves themselves if they reached high enough, could remove Good John from the rock of Dunconnel. Nor was there the slightest danger that the meaningful conversation which they intended to have with him would be interrupted. With characteristic foresight, Lachlan had brought with him a more than adequate supply of food and drink so that their discussions could, if necessary, be prolonged indefinitely. "I am sure," said Lachlan affably, "that Your Majesty will enjoy your stay here." And Good John, as agreeable as ever, meekly assented.

"What we wish to talk to you about," wily Lachlan went on, once they had made themselves comfortable, "is the future; your future and that of the Kingdom of the Isles. That is something which cannot safely be left to chance. You have had a lucky escape from the wiles of Niall MacGillebride Mackinnon. His brother, the Green Abbot, if he should unfortunately survive an attempt which I have every reason to believe will shortly be made on his life, is hardly less dangerous. What Your Majesty needs, it seems to me, is someone you can really trust as your right-hand man — as your deputy, one might almost say."

"You could not do better," interrupted Hector at this point, "than give the job to Lachlan, if, that is, you can induce him to accept it. There's a man who knows what's what. Wily his name and wily his nature, I always say." And he laughed long and loud.

"As Hector says," said Lachlan hastily before Hector could say any more, "I have many commitments, but an appointment I should value and to which I believe I should do justice is that of High Admiral and Lieutenant General of Your Majesty's armed forces. With me in charge, Your Majesty would have no reason to worry your head about routine military matters. Your men would be well armed, well equipped, and well led, your war galleys well manned and seaworthy. And you yourself would be able to give more attention to wider questions of policy and to what I might call the overall strategic concept, at present, in my humble opinion, sadly neglected."

Outside the keep the wind howled still louder and the waves thundered ceaselessly on the rocks, while inside Hector Reaganach continued to finger his battle-axe. Historians, in so far as they have paid much heed to Good John of the Isles, have rated him a realist. Did he not discard his first wife, Amy, and yet cling resolutely to her sizeable inheritance? Being a realist, he did not now see how he could do anything save agree. Accordingly, he agreed.

"I knew all along," said Lachlan Lubanach ingratiatingly, "that once it had been explained to you, a statesman of Your Majesty's experience and vision would readily grasp the advantages of the plan I have ventured to put forward, the importance, above all, of concentrating power in relatively few hands, so long as they are the right hands. To be truly secure, a monarch needs to be well and faithfully served."

"I will drink to that," said Good John promptly with, it seemed to Lachlan, perhaps the slightest touch of irony.

"Now ask him for some land," whispered Hector Reaganach all too audibly.

"Leave it to me, fool," hissed Lachlan back at him under his breath, "and hold your tongue." Then, hoping that the noise of the wind and the waves had drowned this untimely exchange, "There is," he went on in his usual, smoothly compelling tones, "another matter I would be wishing to discuss with Your Majesty, a matter which lies closer to my heart than any question of military honours or barren tracts of land."

"What can he be going to ask for now?" said Good John to himself. "Could it be the Lordship of the Isles? He is more than capable of it."

"I want," said Lachlan, coming suddenly to the point, "your daughter's hand in marriage. She loves me and I love her. Nor, I am sure, would Your Majesty be likely to overlook the advantage which the Kingdom of the Isles would derive from a further strengthening of the bonds of kinship which already so happily unite our two most noble families."

Good John prided himself on being in his homely way a philosopher. A large number of Gaelic and even Latin tags came to mind, endlessly repeated by a wide variety of wiseacres. "In for a penny, in for a pound" was what they added up to. If he wanted to get off Dunconnel alive and retain his sanity, he might as well give Lachlan anything he asked for; it was lucky, all things considered, that he hadn't asked for more. As for Mairi, he had for some time had an idea that the little hussy was up to something. "If my dearest daughter were wishing it," he said, "I would not willingly be withholding my consent."

By now the storm had begun to abate. "With luck," said Lachlan Lubanach, "we may tomorrow be able to set sail for your castle of Ardtornish. Meanwhile, let us drink to Your Majesty's very good health and future prosperity as well as to that of your loyal allies, the Macleans." And he filled to the brim three finely chased silver beakers he had found on board Mackinnon's longboat and promptly appropriated. The coat of arms on them was luckily very similar to his own.

Next day dawned fair and bright. Good John's galley stood in as close to shore as her captain dared, and Good John, wishing he had not drunk quite so much the night before, was rowed out to her in a choppy sea, his new Lord High Admiral and future son-in-law sitting at his side.

But even now the prow of Good John's great galley was not pointed in the hoped-for direction. Instead of a northeasterly, she was following a northwesterly course. "Where are we going now?" he enquired querulously. "Ardtornish is over there." And he pointed in the general direction of the mainland.

"There remains," replied Lachlan obsequiously, "just one small formality for Your Majesty to fulfil. I felt it would be more fitting if, as sovereign and in accordance with ancient tradition, you gave the important decisions you have taken the full force of your royal authority by repeating them when seated on the sacred Black Stone, held in such reverence by your noble fore-fathers. It is for this reason that we have set course for the holy island of Iona, where, as Your Majesty well knows, the sacred stone is situated."

On reaching Iona, the Lord of the Isles found that once again Lachlan's longboat had preceded them. As they came in to land, a group of tonsured ecclesiastics in golden vestments was already awaiting them at the quayside with, at their head, a mitred abbot. Not, he noticed, the Green Abbot, who, he half suspected, had met with a convenient accident, but a mild-look-ing cleric whom he seemed to recognize as some kinsman of Lachlan's. Once Good John had landed, the clergy formed into a procession; at a sign from Lachlan, he himself fell in behind, and, with the abbot leading, the whole party set off in the direction of the Black Stone.

This proved to be an uncompromising-looking block of smooth black basalt which, Good John's atavistic instincts told him, had served similar (and no doubt a number of quite differ-ent) purposes for countless centuries and under a variety of cults. At a gesture from the abbot, Good John seated himself uneasily on the Stone. "Raise your hand," said the abbot, and broke into a Latin chant. Although the exact significance of this escaped him, Good John had the clear impression that an oath was being administered to him, which at the same time enumerated the appalling spiritual and other penalties which would overtake him in the event of his ever going back on his given word, a possibility which, he had to admit, had crossed his mind more than once during the past twenty-four hours. But now there could be no question of his doing so without incurring the absolute certainty of hellfire.

The chant ceased. "Now repeat this after me," said Lachlan, and John, still sitting on the sacred stone, found himself appointing his trusty and well-beloved cousin Lachlan, son of John, son of Gille-Caluim, to be Lord High Admiral and Lieutenant General of the Isles, with what sounded like powers to do anything that entered his head, and, a minute or two later, proclaiming the marriage bans between the said Lachlan and his no less trusty and well-beloved daughter Mairi.

Next came a fresh and not altogether welcome surprise. "I was not," said Lachlan, "wishing to be bothering you with over-many details, but I knew that Your Majesty would naturally be desirous of bestowing on your daughter a suitable dowry. I have accordingly had appended to what has gone before a short list of the lands with which you might most suitably be endowing her and which you will please now be repeating after me."

"A short list..." thought Good John ruefully, as name followed name. Starting with the great castle of Duart, the Black Headland, high on its rock looking out over the Sound of Mull, it seemed, he reflected, to include most of Mull as well as much of the adjacent mainland and practically all the lands formerly held by the now defunct Mackinnon. "How about my own castle of Aros," he wondered. "Will he take that too?"

But Wily Lachlan had almost finished. "For personal reasons, which I am sure Your Majesty will appreciate," he said, "I have just one more request. I would like you to give me the Isles of the Sea and, in addition, appoint me Constable and Captain of your own royal castle of Dunconnel, where together we so successfully consolidated the happy relationship, indeed friendship, which now unites us. For my part, I shall never forget the precious hours we spent there in each other's company."

"No more shall I," said Good John to himself, as he added his signature to a vellum charter which one of the monks, also a Maclean, had pushed in front of him. In the right-hand bottom corner the Great Seal of the Isles, bearing, appropriately enough, a representation of his state galley, was, he noticed, already in place. He could not help wondering just how it had got there, but then, he felt, he would have to become used to surprises with Wily Lachlan as his Lord High Admiral.

Throughout the proceedings, Hector the Ferocious had continued, with difficulty, to hold his tongue, as his elder brother had instructed him to do the previous day. Now he could bear it no longer. "You have forgotten *me*," he said gloomily.

In a flash, Wily Lachlan's expression turned to one of deep reproach. "Your Majesty has forgotten Hector," he said, neatly shifting the blame. Then, after a moment's thought, "Why not give him Lochbuie? It will only take a few minutes to draw up a new charter." And so the fair lands of Lochbuie in their turn passed into Maclean hands.

Wily Lachlan's marriage to Mairi was duly solemnized by the mitred abbot and a baby son born to them not long after, later to become famous as Red Hector of the Battles, a great chief and a great warrior. According to the Seanachie, the young couple's "inclination of yielding" was mutual. This, if anything, was an understatement. The two were deeply devoted and, each being as wily as the other, were blissfully happy together. Indeed, there can be no doubt that Lachlan's love for Mairi had throughout weighed heavily in all his calculations and stratagems. Because of their close blood relationship, a special dispensation was

required from the Vatican for their marriage, but this was readily granted by good Pope Urban who disliked all he had heard of the Green Abbot and his matrimonial excesses, greatly preferring the celibate substitute so promptly provided by Wily Lachlan.

With his new son-in-law at his side, Good John ruled wisely

and well over the Kingdom of the Isles for twenty more years, being, in the fullness of time, succeeded by his son Donald. The more he saw of Lachlan, the more he liked him, finding him a valiant defender, a wise counsellor, and a congenial companion. Thenceforward the Macleans were to be loyal supporters of the House of the Isles against all comers, including on occasion the Scottish Crown. Indeed, it was only relatively late in the day that they finally transferred their allegiance to the House of Stewart.

Of the Mackinnons, less was heard for a time, especially on Mull, but one old chronicler records that some years later one of the Green Abbot's many grandsons, a certain Fyngonius Fyngonii, after acquiring a concubine ("with her mother's full consent"), managed nonetheless to infiltrate himself into the Iona monastery as a monk, subsequently "proceeding to lay violent hands on the goods of the said monastery", including forty cows which he generously made over to his mistress.

On Iain Dubh's death, Lachlan Lubanach succeeded his father as Chief of Clan Maclean, and from his splendid Castle of Duart presided successfully over his clan's affairs for many more years, taking good care when the time came to see that his Oxford-educated brother-in-law Donald of the Isles duly confirmed him in his possession of Duart and his other lands, as well as in his Keepership and Captaincy of Dunconnel.

Duart, Dunconnel, and the other lands on Mull and on the mainland won for the Clan by Lachlan Lubanach, were to remain in Maclean hands for more than three hundred years, the titles and charters first granted by the Lords of the Isles being confirmed by successive Scottish kings. But by the end of the seventeenth century almost all of them, owing to misfortune, occasional misjudgement, but most of all to the clan's unswerving loyalty to the luckless House of Stewart, had passed into the possession of Clan Campbell. It is, however, agreeable to be able to record that in the year 1912 Duart once again became the dwelling place of the Maclean Chiefs, while some seventy years after that the Keepership and Captaincy of the royal castle of Dunconnel were likewise regained for Clan Gillean by the present author, himself a direct descendant of that enterprising warrior, Lachlan the Wily.

Donald The Hunter

IN THE YEAR 1432, Alexander, third Lord of the Isles and King of the Hebrides, lay close to death in the great bed-chamber of his castle at Ardtornish on the Sound of Mull. From all over the Western Highlands and Islands the chiefs and gentlemen of the different clans, who acknowledged him as their over-lord, had come to Ardtornish to pay their respects to the sick man, to satisfy themselves at first hand as to the true state of his health, and to make plans for the future in the case of his demise. Among these was old MacMaster, chieftain of the small clan of that name, which for a hundred years or more had occupied the wild, mountainous region of Ardgour on the shores of Loch Linnhe, fifty or sixty miles farther north. At a time when both were necessary qualities, MacMaster had a reputation for cunning rather than courage, and was widely known in the West Highlands as *An Sionnach*, or the Fox.

The disease which afflicted Alexander was a virulent and debilitating form of dysentery, which had baffled the court physicians and so weakened the sick man that he was now no more than a shadow of his former robust self, lying prone in his great cano-pied bed of state while the attendant court officials and chiefs and gentlemen clustered at a respectful distance in uneasy little groups. This was before the therapeutic virtues of fresh air had been fully recognized by the medical profession. All the windows were tightly closed and heavily curtained, and the atmosphere was painfully fetid.

For all his cunning, the Old Fox was no courtier. After the windswept mountains of Ardgour, the stench of the sickroom

struck disagreeably on his nostrils. Observing Alexander's coma-
tose condition and reckoning that he was as good as dead, he
made no attempt to withold an exclamation of disgust. *"Fuich!"*
he said to those nearest him. And again, *"fuich!"*

But despite the torpor which held him in its grasp, Alexander
was better aware of what was happening around him than he
appeared to be. He heard old MacMaster's *"fuich"* and was displeased by it. This was no way for a mere vassal to behave in the
presence of his sovereign lord. It showed an unacceptable lack of
respect, and the memory of it and of MacMaster's native coarse-
ness lingered and rankled in the sick man's mind.

As Alexander continued to brood over the insult he had
suffered, the door at the farther end of the bedchamber suddenly
opened, and a handsome, vigorous-looking youth burst into the
room, pushing his way through the silent throng, making
straight for Alexander's bedside. Everyone knew who he was.
Donald the Hunter, they called him, son of *Lachlan Bronnach,*
Big-bellied Lachlan, Chief of the Macleans. Equally, everyone

knew that, although Lachlan's eldest son, he had no land of his own and little prospect of ever inheriting any.

Donald's mother was the daughter of Maclean of Kingerloch, who held the lands adjacent to MacMaster's territory of Ardgour, on the shores of nearby Loch Linnhe. Soon after Donald's birth, a score of years earlier, his father, Lachlan Bronnach, had left for the wars with his own father, Red Hector of the Battles, to fight for their cousin Donald of the Isles against the forces of the Scottish Crown assembled near Aberdeen under the command of the King's cousin, Alexander Stewart, Earl of Mar. In the ensuing bloody Battle of Harlaw, Red Hector had died heroically in single combat with the Knight of Drum, while Big-bellied Lachlan, now Chief in his place, had been taken prisoner by Mar.

In due course Lachlan Bronnach was released by his captor, Lord Mar, and returned to his castle of Duart on the Isle of Mull, where he was welcomed home by his adoring family. But somehow his feelings towards Donald's mother seemed to have changed. Although little Donald was there as living proof to the contrary, he began to cast doubts on the entire validity of the arrangement between them, and in the end admitted that he was now affianced to no less a personage than Lord Mar's own daughter; indeed, was about to marry her. Disconsolate, Donald's mother went back to Kingerloch to her father, taking Donald with her, and Lachlan Bronnach married his royal bride. Some time later a son was born to them and recognized by Lachlan as his heir. It now remained to find a role and an inheritance for Donald, who with the years grew up to be a good-looking young man on the best of terms with everyone, connected through his mother as well as through his father with the reigning House of the Isles.

No one was fonder of Donald than his august kinsman Alexander, Lord of the Isles. The mere sight of this cheerful youth, amid so many gloomy, time-serving courtiers, not to mention ill-mannered, devious oafs like old MacMaster, made him feel better. Greeting him warmly, the sick man summoned him to his bedside. Before long, they were deep in talk.

In the Western Highlands, land is the universal topic. Sooner or later every conversation turns to it, and this one was no exception. Alexander was concerned at Donald's landless condition. So, for that matter, was Donald himself, who now pressed his claim as cogently as he could on his cousin, than whom, as both knew, no one was better placed to provide a solution. Throughout Alexander's far-flung dominions all land was held on his authority. Lachlan Bronnach himself held his island territories by virtue of a charter from the Lord of the Isles, and so did the other assembled chiefs and chieftains, including MacMaster of Ardgour, who, observing Alexander's brisker demeanour, was even now wondering uneasily whether his momentary explosion of disgust had not perhaps been untimely. What the Lord of the Isles had given, the Lord of the Isles could take away — there could be no doubt about that.

Already, every man in the great bedchamber was watching Donald as he sat by Alexander and straining his ears to catch what they were saying. Such a conversation could concern any one of them, for better or, more probably, for worse. As Donald rose to take his leave, some of those nearest to him heard Alexander say, *"Leum an garadh far an isle e"*, "Leap the wall where it is lowest", and at the same time saw him cast what they felt was a meaningful glance in the direction of MacMaster.

The significance of what had been said was wasted on no one. An excited buzz went through the room. By now Donald could be seen making for the shore to board his *birlinn*, bound, there could be no doubt, for Loch Linnhe, although whether his likelier landfall would be Kingerloch or Ardgour no one could tell. MacMaster, meanwhile, feeling himself isolated and menaced, was likewise making haste to return home, painfully uncertain what he would find there on his arrival. Some ambiguous words, half warning and half threat, which Donald had flung over his shoulder at him as he left, had done nothing to reassure him.

In fact, Donald was heading as fast as his boat could carry him for Kingerloch. There he gathered a couple of dozen of his grandfather's men at arms and then set out for Ardgour. On reaching Ardgour, the Macleans were fortunate enough to come at once upon MacMaster's infant son. Snatching him from his nurse's arms, they despatched him there and then with their dirks. Their purpose was not simply to chase away the MacMasters but to extirpate them root and branch.

Meanwhile, old MacMaster himself had, on the arrival of the Macleans, made for nearby Corran Ferry in the hope of crossing to the other side before his pursuers could catch up with him. At the ferry he was relieved to see his ferryman, Mac a Charusglaich, fishing from his boat at no great distance from the shore, and called out urgently to him to put him across. But Mac a Charusglaich, continuing to fish, simply remarked that the cuddies were taking well and, when the old man repeated his request with even greater urgency, declared that he seemed to have mislaid his oars, although these, neatly shipped, were clearly visible from the shore.

By now MacMaster was desperate. "Set me across," he shouted, "and I will let you have your croft rent-free in perpetuity."

"Do *you* have the title to *your* land in perpetuity?" came the mocking reply, and MacMaster now knew there was nothing to be done. Already his pursuers could be heard coming nearer. In those days there was a thick wood at Corran, reaching almost to the water's edge, and here he hid himself as best he could, in the hope that, with luck, his pursuers would pass him by.

But he had reckoned without the ferryman. When, not many minutes later, the Macleans arrived at the ferry in hot pursuit, that worthy unshipped his oars and, with long easy strokes, pulled into the shore. "There is an old fox hidden in that wood," he shouted to Donald, and at once the wood was surrounded and old MacMaster dragged out and put to death. The place where he met his end is still marked by a cairn.

"It is a good turn I have done you by refusing to put MacMaster across," said Mac a Charusglaich ingratiatingly to Donald once he had landed. "Now there is no one to dispute your claim."

"That is true," replied Donald, and the ferryman grinned complacently. "But were I situated as he was," Donald continued, "you would quite certainly treat me as you treated him." He then ordered his men to take the ferryman's oars out of his boat and lay them across the lower branches of two trees, so as to make an improvised gallows, on which they proceeded to hang the faithless ferryman without further ado.

At Ardtornish not many months later, a charter was drawn up in due form on vellum, and signed and sealed by Alexander, Lord of the Isles. It bestowed the territory of Ardgour, amounting to more than one hundred thousand acres, on Donald, son of Lachlan, son of Hector, and recognized him, and the heirs of his body in perpetuity, as Chiefs of Ardgour. To this day, just five hundred and fifty years later, Ardgour is still in Maclean hands and likely, I am glad to say, to remain so.

MacNeil's Return to Barra

A T THE TIME of the Norse invasions, the Norsemen came in strength to the island of Barra in the Outer Hebrides and drove out its chieftain, MacNeil, who escaped to Erin. There he remained, and there his children grew up. Years went by, and MacNeil's children, whose father had told them nothing of all this, found that they were still treated as strangers, being known by the Irish as *Barraidich*, or People from Barra. This puzzled them, and one day at dinner they asked their father why they were called by this strange name and what it meant. But their father said only that the word in question caused him the deepest sorrow and begged them never to use it again in his presence. To this they replied, with the painful directness of youth, that they would not eat another mouthful or drink another drop until they knew just what the word meant. And in the end MacNeil relented and told them of all that had happened to him and of the indignity and scorn he had had to endure while the Norsemen lorded it over his lands.

On hearing how they came to be exiles, MacNeil's sons made up their minds to win back their inheritance, and at once began to fit out a *birlinn* to carry them across the seas to Barra. When their vessel had been duly equipped with masts, sails, oars, and a compass, and a proper crew assembled, their father told them to steer straight for Barra Head. There, he said, they would find a man he had left behind on the island, who was still loyal to him. His name was *Mac'illecharaich,* or Macillcary, and he would tell them where they could find their enemies.

When they landed on Barra Head, MacNeil's sons found that

Macillcary was still living there. And when they told him who they were and what they wanted, he advised them to steer for *Bagh-a'Chaisteil,* or Castle Bay, and make for a light that would be showing on the right-hand side of the bay.

On the right-hand side of Castle Bay they came on the house where the light was showing, but they could not gain entrance to it. In the end they climbed on to the roof and, looking through a hole, saw within a poor old man weeping bitterly. When they shouted down to him that they were friends, he let them in and explained that that very day he had paid his rent to the Norsemen and, just because it was a few months short, they had warned him that if he did not bring them the full sum by noon the next day, he would be severely flogged. In return, MacNeil's sons told him of their mission, and the old man joyfully showed them a secret way into the great castle of Kisimul, rising high above the waters of the bay.

Following the old man's instructions, MacNeil's sons were able to take the Norsemen who held the castle by surprise and to kill every one of them. They next went on to the head of the loch and cleared the village of Vaslam of its Norsemen as well. After which they sent word back to their father, who now came to their help with a band of followers. As soon as the news that MacNeil had landed reached them, all the natives of the island who were loyal to him hastened to join him.

But the MacNeils' task was only half finished. By an inlet at the northern end of the island another stronghold, known as Eoligarry Castle, was still held in strength by the Norsemen. As it happened, there was amongst the islanders who had joined MacNeil, an unacknowledged son of his who had stayed behind in the island and who, from the circumstances of his birth, was known as *Mac-an-Amharuis,* or the Son of Doubt. Mac-an-Amharuis now called on MacNeil to recognize him as a son. To this his putative father replied, "If you are really a son of mine, prove it by clearing the whole island of my enemies before morning."

"Give me the means then," said Mac-an-Amharuis, "and there will not be a trace of a Norseman on the island." And MacNeil gave him his own sword.

That night, when the Norsemen, who had been carousing heavily, were sound asleep, Mac-an-Amharuis crept secretly into the castle and killed them all where they lay. And it is said that to this day, when a great storm sweeps the sand hither and thither over the fortress where they were slain, their bones can still be seen lying on the sea floor, washed white by the waves. As for Mac-an-Amharuis, MacNeil now proudly acknowledged him as his son, saying, with fatherly pride, that only a true MacNeil could have performed such heroic deeds.

"And from that day," says the Seanachie, "MacNeil had his rights." That some of his descendants sought to encroach on the rights of others and received their just deserts may be seen from the next tale.

Maclean's Return to Coll

A GREAT MANY YEARS AGO, Maclean of Duart, while on his way by boat to collect the rents from his lands on Tiree, put in at Kelis on the Isle of Coll, then held by the Norsemen, to see if he could buy any meat. But the woman of the house to which he sent for the meat, who was herself a Maclean, replied that in her view he was not worth providing with meat. Whereat Duart, intrigued, came ashore himself to enquire, in a friendly manner, what her reason could be for saying this. Her reason, she replied with great frankness, was simply that he had not had the courage to take Coll for his own clan, as he should have done long ago. Should he ever change his mind, she, for her part, could offer him thirty men of her own, who would always be at his disposal if he needed help.

This made Duart think that perhaps Coll should, after all, be in Maclean hands rather than in the hands of the Norsemen. Accordingly, an expedition was mounted and the Norsemen driven out, after which, at Duart's insistance, a charter was drawn up by his kinsman, the Lord of the Isles, bestowing the island on a member of Duart's own family, as Chieftain of Coll. Some years later, the First Maclean of Coll died, leaving a little son, Iain, only a few months old. Not long after this, his widow married MacNeil of Barra as her second husband.

MacNeil's first act, following his marriage, was to establish himself on Coll and to send little Iain to his own island of Barra in the charge of a nurse. On Barra the nurse soon found herself a lover, who, being a local man, knew all the gossip. The gossip, she quickly learned, was that MacNeil intended to have his stepson done away with, so that he could himself take possession of

Coll in addition to Barra. The nurse, a loyal Maclean, accordingly decided to leave Barra immediately, taking her lover and little Iain with her.

They left by night in a two-oared coracle, but it was not long before they saw that they were being pursued by MacNeil's great eight-oared galley with a steersman at the helm. The nurse and her lover rowed as hard as they could, but soon the galley was gaining on them fast. Both boats were making for the narrow sound between Sorisdale and Boust. By this time, it was *beir's cha bheir,* overtake or not overtake. Everything depended on who got there first. When the two boats reached the narrows, with now only a few feet between them, the little coracle shot safely through and escaped, but the long oars of the galley were shattered against the rocky walls of the narrows, since when the place has been known as *Caolas 'Bhriste-Ramh,* the Strait of the Broken Oars.

From Barra the fugitives, having thrown off their pursuers, made for Mull, whence, under Duart's protection, little Iain was sent to Erin, well out of the reach of his stepfather. There the boy grew to be a fine, big, handsome man, earning the name of *Iain Garbh* or Sturdy Iain. One day Iain Garbh told the Irishwoman with whom he was lodging that that night he had dreamed of a pile of oatcakes and of a drip of water from the roof that had fallen on the oatcakes and gone right through them. To this the Irishwoman, who had the second sight, replied that his dream meant that he was by rights the owner of land and in time would get back what was due to him. Encouraged by this, Iain Garbh returned to Mull and there gathered some men with whom to land on Coll. One of these was a swarthy, bald-headed fellow from Dervaig, known as *Gille Riabhach,* the Grizzled Lad. Six of the others also came from Dervaig. Before leaving, all of them, as though to set the tone for their expedition, swore solemnly on their dirks to kill the first human being they encountered after landing on the island.

On reaching Coll, Iain Garbh, while making a preliminary reconnaissance, came upon his old foster-mother gathering mussels on the shore. She had aged a lot and seemed unhappy. *"Dia le Macilleathain,"* "God be with Maclean," he heard her mumbling. "More pity that Maclean is not alive," for she did not recognize him.

"What were you saying?" asked Iain Garbh.

"Conceal what I said," she replied hastily, for she was afraid. "Women say many foolish things."

Then he revealed to her who he was, and when the Grizzled Lad and his companions caught up with him and declared that they must kill her in accordance with their vow, he firmly ordered them to desist.

It had, the old woman now said, long been foretold on the island that Maclean would return. In anticipation of this, MacNeil, who was now living at Grisipol House, would every day send a servant on a white horse for news to Breacachadh, where the boats usually landed. If all was well, the messenger would return slowly, facing his horse's rump. If there was anyone accompanying him, his companion, if a friend, was obliged to walk on the right of the horse, while a stranger was made to walk on the left. That very day, she told them, MacNeil's messenger had just left Breacachadh and was now on his way back to Grisipol.

On learning this, Iain Garbh and his companions immediately ran to the top of the nearest hill, whence they could see the messenger riding slowly along on his white horse, placidly facing the beast's tail. There was no one with him. Iain Garbh at once offered a generous reward to the first man to intercept him.

"I," said the Grizzled Lad, "will do it, if you will give me my croft at Dervaig rent-free."

Impatiently, Iain agreed, for time was of the essence, but the Grizzled Lad was still not satisfied. "Words are great," he said, "but solemn oaths are better." Nor would he move a yard until Iain had sworn solemnly by all he held most sacred to let him have his croft free of rent.

The Grizzled Lad then set off and, running rapidly across country, reached a point on the road some way ahead of the messenger. Crouching by the side of the road and pretending to be a beggar, he started to search his clothes for lice while the messenger came nearer. When the latter finally came up with him, the Grizzled Lad asked him civilly enough where MacNeil was, and was told, at Grisipol House. Whereupon, he immediately leapt up on the horse behind the messenger and stabbed him to death with his dirk.

After Iain Garbh and the others had come up with the Grizzled Lad, they set out together for Grisipol House, where MacNeil and his wife, happily unaware of Iain Garbh's arrival on the island, were at dinner.

Once MacNeil had dined, it was customary for a herald to make the following proclamation, "Hear, all ye people, and hark, all ye nations! The great MacNeil of Barra having finished his dinner, the princes of the earth may now dine." For once, however, this ceremony was dispensed with. The non-appearance of the messenger had already been noticed, and now a serving man, known as the Black Lad, came rushing in with the news that strangers were approaching, at which Lady MacNeil, looking out of the window, observed that one of them looked remarkably like her son Iain.

It did not take MacNeil long to sum up the situation. Announcing, a trifle superfluously, that wartime was no time for sleeping, he rushed out to give battle, with the Black Lad following him, carrying a great battle axe, and the rest of his retainers hard on their heels.

During the fight that followed, the Grizzled Lad, hard pressed by MacNeil's Black Lad, suddenly took a great leap backwards

and upwards across the burn that runs past Grisipol House, thus avoiding a savage blow from the Black Lad's axe, which, narrowly missing him, buried itself in the ground. This gave the Grizzled Lad his chance. Before the Black Lad could recover the axe, he was on him like a flash and, snatching it up, cut the Black Lad's head clean off with it. To this day the place where this happened is known as *Leum a' Ghille Riabhaich,* the Grizzled Lad's Leap.

Meanwhile, with his feet in the sea at the mouth of the burn, Iain Garbh was battling manfully with his stepfather. At this moment the Grizzled Lad came running up. "I want to be honest with you, MacNeil," he shouted a little unconvincingly, as he laid about him with the Black Lad's battle axe. "They are creeping up on you from behind." At which MacNeil foolishly turned his head, and the Grizzled Lad, delighted at the success of his simple stratagem, cut it off with a single blow. Thereafter, the rest of MacNeil's men were quickly cornered and killed in a nearby hollow, still known as *Glaic nan cnamh,* the Hollow of the Bones.

Once the fighting was over, Iain Garbh's mother, again a widow, came out of Grisipol House to greet him. In her arms she carried her youngest child and in her sweetest tones bade Sturdy Iain look at his young brother smiling at him. For a moment Iain grinned back, then, drawing his dirk, he stabbed the child to death in their mother's arms. As the Grizzled Lad kept repeating with homely wisdom, there could be no advantage in sparing a child who in time might well seek to avenge his father's death.

In this manner was the Isle of Coll restored to the possession of its rightful owners.

The Last Hanging;
A Tale of Tiree

THE MARRIED LIFE of Lachlan Cattanach, eleventh Chief of Clan Maclean, in regard to whom even Maclean seanachies have reservations, was, to say the least of it, full of incident. As his first wife he married the Lady Elizabeth Campbell, sister of Colin, Earl of Argyll. But, although encouraged by the bride's brother, who saw in it a possible means of gaining possession of Maclean's lands, which he had long coveted, the match was not a happy one. Not only did the bride, at any rate according to Maclean sources, include in her retinue a young lover thinly disguised as a monk and loudly object when Lachlan insisted on sleeping with a sharp sword at his side, she also, it appears, tried to poison her husband, using for this purpose the then little-known drug *cavale*. Last but not least, despite Lachlan's best endeavours, she did not present him with the heir he had hoped for. Accordingly, Lachlan decided to get rid of her, his method being to leave her on a low rock in the Sound of Mull, known to this day as the Lady's Rock, which at high tide would, if all went well, be covered by the waves. What he could scarcely have foreseen was that, shortly after he had left her there, Elizabeth's two brothers would be passing that way in their *birlinn* or that, when he arrived that evening to dine with them, loudly lamenting his sad loss, he would find himself seated next to his wife at table — by any standards an awkward situation. Their marriage, needless to say, did not survive this unhappy episode although Lachlan somewhat suprisingly did.

Still undeterred, Lachlan next married another Campbell, Margaret, daughter of Campbell of Achinbreck, but she, too, proved barren. In despair, he now turned to his own clan, taking as his third wife Marian, the handsome and lively daughter of Maclean of Treshnish, Captain of Cairnburgh. By Marian, Lachlan managed to have two sturdy sons, Hector and Allan. Nor did she object to his sleeping with a sword at his side. Nor seek to poison him. It was not long, however, before he began to have grave doubts about her fidelity.

The truth of the matter was that, while they were living at Island House on the Isle of Tiree, Marian had become enamoured of an Irish chieftain named William O'Buie, who warmly reciprocated her feelings. In those days, there was a good deal of traffic between Ireland and the Western Isles, and a lively correspondence sprang up between the lovers. Having intercepted one of O'Buie's letters to his wife, Lachlan Cattanach was, says the Seanachie, "much distressed about this injury to his honour". To test his wife's real feelings, he showed her a pen-knife which he had also intercepted, saying, "This is a present O'Buie has sent you." To which she replied insultingly, and in rhyming couplets:

"My darling, who sent me the knife,
I weary at his delay in coming across the sea.
And may I not enjoy health,
If I do not love it better than the hand that now holds it."

This told Lachlan Cattanach all he needed to know. Summoning his notoriously resourceful kinsman and neighbour Lachlan Fionn or Fair Lachlan, he said to him, "You are a clever man and have seven sons. Go to Ireland and bring me back O'Buie's head and I will thereafter overlook any crime you may commit."

Excited by this generous offer, Lachlan Fionn and his sons at once set out for Ireland in their galley. They reached Islay before sundown, and next day were in Ireland. On arriving there, Lachlan Fionn asked the first man he met where he could find William O'Buie.

"Should it be your wish to see him," replied the Irishman, "he will soon be after coming this way in a coach drawn by a pair of white horses. And no one in all Ireland has that but himself."

So Lachlan Fionn continued along the road in the direction the man had shown him, and after a while met O'Buie's coach with the white horses, coming towards him.

On catching sight of Lachlan Fionn, O'Buie ordered him to stop. "I see you are a stranger in these parts," he said.

"Yes," said Lachlan Fionn.

"Whence have you come?" asked O'Buie.

"From the Isle of Tiree," replied Lachlan Fionn.

"Do you know the Lady of Maclean there?" enquired O'Buie.

"I know her well."

"Will you bring her a message from me?"

"Certainly," said Lachlan Fionn. Whereupon O'Buie, having written out an affectionate message, put his head out of the coach to hand the note to Lachlan Fionn, who, taking the message with one hand, quickly struck off O'Buie's head with the other. Then, taking the head with him, he made for his galley as fast as he could go. That evening he was in Islay, and next day back on Tiree.

As soon as he had landed, Lachlan Fionn went to Island House. Finding Maclean and his wife at breakfast, he placed O'Buie's head on the table, facing Lady Maclean, who, when she saw it, let out a shriek and fell down dead. In this manner

Maclean's honour had been abundantly satisfied; Lachlan Fionn had more than justified the confidence put in him and fully deserved the promised exemption from punishment for any crime he might now choose to commit.

Not long afterwards, Lachlan Fionn's sons were taking home peat from Mors to Hynish on Tiree. There were five of them, with seven horses carrying baskets of peat. At that time there was a mill at Balvicem with a bridge across the dam which was lifted at sundown and which on their way home they had to cross. That evening, the sons of Lachlan Fionn had worked longer and harder than they had intended and had stopped by the way to partake of refreshment. It was therefore well past sundown when they reached the bridge and it had already been drawn up. But, with the quantity of whisky they had drunk and at the speed they were going, they did not notice this and, before they could stop, the leading horse of their team had fallen headlong into the dam and been choked.

When they reached home, the lads told their father how the miller had pulled up the bridge at nightfall and what had happened. At this, Lachlan Fionn flew into a rage and, remembering the exemption from punishment he had earned from Lachlan Cattanach, said to his sons, "If my horse was choked on the miller's account, he will himself meet the very same fate tonight." And so, making their way to the mill and finding the miller asleep in bed, Lachlan and his sons took him and hanged him on the Hillock of the Cross, just across the way from Island House.

Early next morning Lachlan Cattanach's serving man came as usual to wake his master and kindle the fire in his room before he rose from his bed. As usual, the Chief asked him what kind of day it was. To this the servant replied that it was a fine enough day, but that there was a strange sight to be seen.

"And what would that be?" asked the Chief.

"It is a man hanged on the hillock up yonder," was the reply.

This angered Maclean, who had a strong sense of the proprieties. It was not that he objected to hanging as such; he just would not have people hanged on the island without his authority. "Who or what person dared do this without my permision?" he asked, climbing irritably out of bed. But then, all at once, he understood that this must be the work of Lachlan Fionn, and he shed tears of rage. "It was," he said sadly, "part of the agreement I made with him when he brought me the man's head from Ireland."

"And this," says the Seanachie, "was the last hanging that was done in the island." Strangely enough, this distressing incident had put Lachlan Cattanach off hanging altogether.

The eleventh Chief of Clan Maclean died, as the saying goes, in his bed, stabbed there while on a visit to Edinburgh in 1527 by his first wife's brother, John Campbell of Calder, acting on behalf of his elder brother, the Earl of Argyll, who, some said, still resented Lachlan's unsuccessful attempt thirty years earlier to drown their sister. Others maintain that the Campbells acted from political motives, or, no less probably, from a perennial desire to get their hands on as much Maclean territory as they could; an aim in which they were eventually to be all too successful.

Clara's Well

IN A SHELTERED CORNER of the green isle of Lismore, looking out across the Sound of Mull, there rises a clear spring of water which to this day bears the name *Tobar a Clar,* Clara's Well. How it came by that name is a tale still told in the Western Highlands.

Of the Armada of one hundred and thirty Spanish ships that set sail from the mouth of the Tagus river in May 1588, under the command of the Duke of Medina Sidonia, none was more majestic or better equipped than the great galleon *Florencia,* endowed, it is said, by the Grand Duke of Tuscany himself. Her rows of heavy cannon were well suited for blasting an enemy at close quarters; her noble captain, Don Fareija, was renowned alike for his seamanship and his courage; while the men at arms and seamen serving under him were worthy of their commander and as confident as he that victory awaited them in their forthcoming encounter with the naval forces of Spain's bitterest enemy, Queen Elizabeth of England.

There was, however, at least one member of the ship's company whom the Duke of Medina Sidonia would have been astonished to meet, had he chanced to visit the *Florencia* in person. The mighty castle that towered above the galleon's decks, with its rows of magnificently carved and gilded portholes, contained ample space for more than one luxuriously appointed cabin, and of these the most luxurious of all had been set aside for a mysterious passenger, muffled in a great black sea cloak and smuggled aboard under cover of darkness only a few hours before sailing time. It was not until the next day, when they were already well out to sea, that the *Florencia*'s seamen, looking up from their labours, might have become aware of a slight, auburn-haired figure in a sea cloak, high above them on the quarterdeck, gazing fixedly out across the waves.

Just who this mysterious passenger was, Don Fareija alone could have said, but to the great frustration of both officers and crew, he kept his secret to himself. A week or two earlier, while more than usually busy with his duties as captain, he had been privately summoned to the Escorial and there entrusted with a mission which, to the captain of a ship preparing for early action, was, to say the least of it, unwelcome. After a lengthy and not always very relevant preamble, it had been explained to him by a flustered privy councillor that, of late, Doña Clara, the dazzlingly beautiful sixteen-year-old daughter of a second cousin of King Philip, had become very difficult, in fact impossible, to deal with. Not to put too fine a point on it, she seemed possessed.

Doña Clara's recently widowed father, a fussy, ineffectual princeling, who for practical purposes had always relied in such situations on his handsome red-haired wife, was at his wits' end. Her confessor, a suave, worldly-wise member of the newly founded Order of Jesus, who in the ordinary way should have been more than capable of dealing with teenage tantrums, had likewise admitted himself baffled. The court physician equally. The mother superior of the convent to which difficult royal princesses were usually consigned let it be known that, although an old friend of the family, she would sooner not admit Doña Clara to her well-ordered establishment.

The truth of the matter was that for some months now Clara had been subject to visions, one might almost say visitations. These came to her at night with a force which she would have found irresistible, had she felt any desire to resist. Night after night, after retiring to her maidenly couch with its chaste white curtains and coverlets, she would awake, or seem to awake so violent were her sensations, in the arms of a tall, strongly built, blue-eyed, tawny-haired man of thirty. This was no airy fantasy, but physical reality, compared with which her waking hours had come to have but little meaning, least of all the time she was obliged to spend with her affianced, a weedy young grandee of

Spain, who, although entitled to wear his hat in the royal presence, had little else to recommend him. With time, substance and shadow had mingled irretrievably. Her dreams had become the only reality in her life, one by comparison with which everything else was meaningless.

Her lover, for that was how she had come to regard him, was not, she knew, a Spaniard. He came, as far as she could judge, from some northern clime, a land of mists and vapours, of brown hills and green meadows, grey rocks and dark headlands. Such was the background to her dreams. Of his existence she was as certain as she was of her own, of which he had become the most important part. All her hopes, her energies, her aspirations were directed towards one aim — to find him and spend the rest of her life with him. Little wonder that those closest to her found her hard to live with.

Needless to say, it was not usual for Spanish ships of the line to carry female passengers, least of all in wartime. But to those most immediately concerned the *Florencia's* forthcoming departure seemed to offer a happy solution to their difficulties. The Spaniards looked forward to a quick, easy victory over the English. After that, the Armada would doubtless put in at one or two northern ports before returning home in triumph. To Clara, in her present mood, it seemed a direct answer to her prayers. Her father, her spiritual adviser, and the mother superior of the convent, all devoutly anxious to be rid of her for a spell, saw things in much the same light. Even her physician advanced the view that a prolonged sea voyage might prove beneficial to her health. And so strings were pulled, the necessary arrangements were made, Don Fareija received his instructions, and a fine May morning some weeks later found Doña Clara, with the breeze in her auburn hair, watching the sunlit domes and towers of Lisbon fast receding into the distance.

Doña Clara's journey was to prove longer and more full of incident than she or anyone else could have foreseen. Scarcely had they left Lisbon than the King of Spain's ships ran into storms which utterly destroyed two of their number and forced the rest to put into Corunna to refit. It was July before they set sail a second time, bound for the English Channel. In the Narrow

Seas they found the English waiting to engage them. In the ensuing action, the cumbrous Spanish galleons suffered severely at the hands of the lighter, swifter, more easily manoeuvrable English craft. The weather was once more against them. "The winds of God," the Spaniards called the shifting winds which so often worked against them, laying the blame for their defeat fairly and squarely at the door of the Almighty, while the English, for their part, generously allowed a Protestant Deity to share the credit for their victory over the Most Christian King.

To the Duke of Medina Sidonia, already a sick man, one thing at least was clear. There could be no question of his ships returning to Spain by the route they had followed on the voyage out; they had had more than enough of the Narrow Seas, now more securely than ever in English hands. They must sail northwards and, braving the autumn gales, make their way home as best they could by way of the far north of Scotland and Ireland, inhospitable regions full of unknown perils.

For King Philip, on his knees half the day in his private chapel in the Escorial; for the Duke of Medina Sidonia, ailing in his cabin; for thousands of hard-pressed Spanish seamen and soldiers in their storm-tossed galleons, the outlook was, to say the least of it, disheartening. But for Doña Clara, single-minded as only a woman in love can be, none of these things possessed the slightest significance when set against the purpose of her quest. Although battered by shot and shell and stormy seas, the *Florencia* was still afloat and now, it seemed, was at long last heading for those misty regions in the far northwest which served as the background to her dearest dreams.

There is no complete record of the *Florencia*'s long journey northwards, skirting up the east coasts of England and Scotland, or how she rounded Cape Wrath, before threading her way southwards through the crag-studded, gale-wracked waters of the Western Approaches. All we know for certain is that on a blustery autumn morning in September 1588 she finally dropped anchor in the bay of *Tobar Mhoire* or Tobermory, Mary's Well, on the Isle of Mull in the Inner Hebrides.

*   *   *   *

For more than two centuries the Isle of Mull had been a strong-hold of the Macleans, whose chiefs, now at the height of their power, ruled over it and over much of the adjoining mainland from their castle of Duart, perched high on its rocky promontory above the Sound of Mull. At this time the Chief of Clan Maclean was Lachlan Mor, Lachlan the Great, fourteenth of his line, renowned throughout the Highlands and beyond both as a statesman and as a warrior, brave as a lion and, at the age of thirty, wise and resourceful beyond his years. Physically, he was an impressive figure, well over six feet tall and broad in propor-tion, with tawny hair, high cheekbones, and deep-set blue eyes that showed the Viking blood far back in his ancestry.

It did not take long for news of the galleon's arrival to reach Duart. That the *Florencia* flew the Spanish flag or that Spain was at war with Scotland's southern neighbour England, did not greatly concern Lachlan. He had had dealings, it is true, with the English queen, just as he had had dealings, not always friendly, with her cousin, King James VI of Scotland, whose authority he recognized when it suited him to do so. First and foremost, he was Chief of Clan Maclean, an independent ruler with plenty of problems of his own.

At the moment, the problem which concerned Lachlan Mor most was his feud with his neighbours and close relatives, the MacDonalds, for centuries the allies of the Macleans, but now their rivals and bitter enemies. What he needed were arms and men with which to fight them. To him, then, the news that a Spanish warship, bristling with cannon and packed with men at arms, was anchored off Tobermory signified a heaven-sent opportunity to recruit well-armed allies to join him in his struggle against the detestable MacDonalds. Calling for his horse, a shaggy Highland garron, he at once galloped off to Tobermory, and some hours later was being rowed out to the *Florencia* in his state barge, his chief's standard flying from the stern.

Don Fareija, or Captain Forester as he is known to this day in Mull, had found, greatly to his relief, that the natives were inclined to be friendly. He himself had the naturally courteous manners of a Spanish nobleman. Recognizing in Lachlan Mor a kindred spirit whose regard for good breeding was no less than his own, he treated him with the deference which his high station demanded, a deference which Lachlan, it must be said, sometimes found lacking in the Lowlands, where, it seemed to him, there was little understanding of such things. In French of a kind, helped out by the odd word of dog Latin, they found a common language. Sitting at ease at the great mahogany table in Don Fareija's splendid cabin, drinking from gilded goblets a rare sherry from that worthy's own vineyards, it was not long before the two of them had arrived at a mutually satisfactory agreement: so many cannon and the services of so many gunners, pikemen and musketeers in return for a safe anchorage, so many cattle and sheep, and so many hogsheads of grain.

In matters of hospitality Spaniards can hold their own with Highlanders. Just as Lachlan Mor was about to suggest that they adjourned to Duart to partake of further refreshment, a great gong sounded, and Don Fareija led his guest to another, even more magnificent cabin, where three places were laid for dinner. Then, while Lachlan was asking himself who their companion was to be, the cabin door opened, and, looking up, he caught sight of the most beautiful woman he had ever seen, in whose dazzling appearance there was at the same time something strangely familiar, a likeness to someone he felt he already knew. Surely in some half-remembered dream or waking fantasy he had already seen that slender body, that great mass of auburn hair, those delicate features, those green eyes, that pale, translucent skin. As she entered the cabin, her eyes, too, lit up with an answering look of recognition, and he knew in a flash that this was the great love of his life.

For what occurred next, it seems best to turn to the traditional Gaelic version of the tale, as handed down on Mull over the centuries by successive seanachies, from one generation to the next. "She clasped her hands round his neck and kissed him," runs the Gaelic text, "and so she fell in with the gentleman she had seen in her vision or dream. And Maclean stopped with her for several days."

News travels fast on Mull. Twelve years earlier, Lachlan Mor had married Lady Margaret Cunninghame, daughter of the Earl of Glencairn, a Lowland nobleman of great possessions; not so great, however, as those of the even nobler Earl of Atholl, whose daughter and sole heiress Lachlan had, amid great indignation, thrown over to marry Margaret. Although much attached to her husband, Margaret, a hard-headed Lowlander, had few illusions about him. Had she not herself, after all, won him away from his affianced bride in the course of some light-hearted banter around the card table about how you cut for partners, and why? What she had done, others could do also. An old ballad well describes her dilemma:

A lady has come from the green sunny bowers
Of a far southern clime, to the mountains of ours;
A light in her eyes, but deceit in her heart,
And she lingers, and lingers, and will not depart.

Through darkness and danger, 'mid tempest and rain,
She has sail'd to our shores from the vineyards of Spain,
Forsaking her country, her kindred, her home,
Abroad through our cold Western Islands to roam,
To find a young lover as fair to her sight
As a vision she saw in the slumbers of night.

And hither by stars inauspicious convey'd,
She has come, in her gems and her beauty array'd,
With a tongue full of sweetness, a heart insincere,
And fixed her bright eyes on the Chief of Maclean,
To toy with his heart, and bewilder his brain.

And I, who was once the delight of his soul,
Ere she like a blight on my happiness stole,
Now wander through Duard, neglected and 'lorn,
Of a stranger the scoff, of my maidens the scorn;
With a grief in my bosom that gnaws at the core,
And a fire in my brain that will burn evermore.

Learning after several days that Lachlan was still on board the *Florencia* and what kept him there, and not wishing to see her happy, well-ordered domestic life disrupted by any dream-

maiden from Spain, the Lady of Duart decided on drastic action. In Lachlan's kinsman, Donald Glas, or Grey Donald, of Morvern, she found a ready helper. Him she now despatched to the galleon with a message to Lachlan to say that she wished to see him on shore at his earliest convenience. After delivering his message to Lachlan and seeing him safely into his longboat, Donald Glas, as one seafaring man to another, engaged the galleon's master gunner in conversation. It would, he said, interest him to see the ship's powder magazine. Nothing, replied the Spaniard courteously, could be easier.

Once in the powder magazine, Donald knew exactly what to do. Waiting until the old gunner's back was turned, he lighted a length of slow-burning fuse he had brought with him, and then, declaring his Chief had urgent need of him, went over the side in a hurry. He was halfway back to the shore when the galleon blew up and sank with all hands, including, there could sadly be no doubt, the fair Doña Clara. The only survivor was a solitary dog belonging to one of the sailors, which, blown high into the air, landed safe and sound on shore and for months thereafter sat howling by the bay, opposite the spot where the galleon and his master had gone down. Lady Margaret had acted in the nick of time. "Maclean," reports the bard, "was intending to go away with the princess, for he had become as fond of her as she was of him."

A few days after the explosion, Clara's body, carried there by the currents, was washed up on the green island of Lismore, across the Sound of Mull. Her face was paler in death, some strands of seaweed had caught in her long auburn hair, and her clothing clung closely to her youthful body. Sadly, Lachlan, crossing from Mull, buried her where she lay, by the shore, not far from the ancient shrine of Saint Moluaig.

But Doña Clara was not to rest in peace. One night, a year or two later, when Lady Margaret was away visiting her noble relatives in the south, Lachlan, lying alone in the darkness in his great bedchamber at Duart, suddenly became aware with mingled ecstasy and fear of a pale, auburn-haired presence by his side and of a cold hand laid upon his. "Do not," she said, "leave my bones to lie alone any longer on Lismore, but take them, cleanse them carefully in the waters of the little spring that rises by the holy shrine of Saint Moluaig, and carry them back to my father in far-off Spain." And so, making some excuse to his wife, "all this," says the Seanachie, "he did. Maclean washed her bones in the well, and the well is to this day named *Tobar a Clar*, Clara's Well. . . . And Maclean sailed for Spain with her remains and delivered them to her father."

Clara Ivert

115

Here, one could have thought, this sad little tale might have ended. But fate, we learn, decreed otherwise. "On examining Clara's remains," says the Seanachie, "her father was greatly distressed to find one of her joints amissing and, falling into a rage, ordered two of his best galleons to destroy the island of Mull and Maclean with it." It is also possible that the Spaniards were angered by the close understanding which had of late grown up between Lachlan Mor and Spain's deadly enemy, Elizabeth of England. However this may be, on getting wind of what was afoot, Lachlan Mor, a resourceful man, prepared for trouble. In such an emergency he knew that he could count on the help of his loyal allies, the *Doideagan Muileach* or Grizzled Ones of Mull, in other words, the witches for whom the island had long been famous and who, as prominent members of his clan, proudly acclaimed him as their chief. Of these, none could cast more potent spells than Big Gormsuil, who dwelt on lofty Ben Mor, the highest of all the hills on Mull, and who, with her weird companions, now came loyally to Lachlan's aid.

As soon as the galleons hove into sight, the witches set about raising a terrible storm, while repeatedly dunking in a bath tub two small replicas of the Spanish craft. But the Spaniards, who, it appeared, had a witch of their own on board, fought back, matching spell with counter-spell. "The wind," recounts the Seanachie, "blew a hurricane from the Castle . . . while the witches, in the shape of crows, perched on the galleons' mastheads."

At this juncture there was a flash of lightning and a clap of thunder and Big Gormsuil herself, swooping down from Ben Mor in the guise of an immense black cat, clung with her claws to the masthead of the larger galleon. "Then," says the Seanachie, "the Spanish captain gave up all hope, and the ships began to drive before the storm. The Spaniards got their axes out to cut away the foremast, but the heads of the axes flew off the shafts and over the side. And the two galleons drove ashore at the back of Lismore and sank. And all hands perished."

Duncan's Cairn

BESIDE THE ROAD between Kilchoman and *Traigh
Ghruinnaird* on the island of Islay stands a pile of stones
known as Cairnduncan or Duncan's Cairn. How it came by that
name is a story still told by the people who dwell thereabouts.

Of all the chiefs of Clan Maclean few won greater fame as
warriors than Sir Lachlan Mor, fourteenth of Duart. Indeed,
towards the end of his life, perhaps to help him forget the lovely
princess from Spain, who for a few fleeting days had meant more
to him than anything else, he spent most of his time fighting.
"The life he had been leading," says the clan historian, without
going into greater detail, "made him restless and the desire for
war grew upon him." In October 1594, wearing chain mail and
wielding an immense, double-headed, Danish battle-axe, he
performed prodigies of valour at the Battle of Glenlivet, fighting
for King James against the Catholic earls of Angus, Huntly and
Errol, whose aim it had been to restore the old religion in
Scotland. Next, he offered his services to Queen Elizabeth of
England, whose hold on Ireland was at the time seriously threatened by O'Neill, the insurgent Earl of Tyrone, who had
managed to enlist against her the support of both Spain and the
Pope. In return for Lachlan's help, the English Queen sent him
what he calls in a letter to Sir Robert Cecil, "an honorable token
of her favour," namely a thousand crowns, a welcome addition to
his permanently depleted coffers.

But from start to finish, Lachlan Mor's real quarrel was with
the MacDonalds. In 1596 King James VI, angered by some
dastardly MacDonald outrage and temporarily well disposed

towards the Macleans, had confirmed the latters' title to the Rhinns of Islay, some strategically situated lands on the island, commanding the trade route to Ireland and for some time bitterly disputed between the two clans. This decision the Mac-Donalds had stubbornly refused to accept. By now, Lachlan's nephew, James MacDonald of Islay, his sister Mary's son, had become Chief of Clan Donald. In the summer of 1598, after much bickering, Lachlan Mor agreed, not without misgivings, to meet his nephew on Islay and discuss the matter. To say that neither party trusted the other would be an understatement. Though there was some talk of negotiation, it must have been clear from the first that an armed clash was the more probable outcome.

Ever since they had saved him from destruction at Spanish hands ten years earlier, it had been Lachlan's practice to consult his witches, the *Doideagan Muileach*, before setting out on any important enterprise. This time, they warned him, first, on no account to land on Islay on a Thursday; secondly, not to drink from a well known as *Tobar Neill Neonaich* or Weird Neil's Well; and, thirdly, not to fight a battle at *Traigh Ghruinnaird*, that is, on the shores of Loch Gruinnard.

Before setting out for Islay, Lachlan took another step which was perhaps less than prudent. For previous generations of Maclean chiefs it had been the custom, when leaving for the wars, to walk in procession thrice clockwise, that is, with the sun, round a little island in Loch Spelvie on Mull, in order to invoke divine support. Although this must surely have been a pre-Christian tradition, Lachlan, an early and enthusiastic convert to Protestantism, now decided to show his contempt for what he conceived as popery by walking thrice round the island in the contrary direction, widdershins.

The date on which he had decided to land on Islay with a force of several hundred clansman was Wednesday, 4th August. But weather in the Western Isles is at the best uncertain. On the way over from Mull, a storm blew up, and it was not until the following morning that the Macleans were able to go ashore. Nor did the storm leave Lachlan with any choice where to land. Approaching Islay from the west, his *birlinn* ran before the wind, right into the relative shelter of Loch Gruinnard. Securely entrenched in a strong position on some high ground above the shore, the MacDonalds were waiting for him. There could be no doubt as to their hostile intentions or as to the site of the now inevitable battle, namely the shore of Loch Gruinnard. It was a swelteringly hot August day, and Lachlan, toiling uphill in his chain mail, felt thirsty. Someone gave him a drink of cool water which he swallowed without thinking. On asking the name of the spring it came from, he was told: *Tobar Neill Neonaich.*

And now, as Lachlan Mor was preparing for battle under these unhappy auspices, he was approached by a strange, dusky, stunted little creature known as *Dubh Sith,* the Black Elf, said to be the son of a fairy woman and of a man called Shaw from the neighbouring island of Jura. Explaining that he was a skilled archer and, as a native of Jura, a loyal supporter of Clan Maclean, he offered Lachlan Mor his services. His appearance was unprepossessing and his manner unconvincing. Haughtily, Lachlan rejected him, saying that he had plenty of bowmen of his own and did not need a little runt like him. At which Dubh Sith went off, scowling, to offer his services to the MacDonalds, and shortly afterwards battle was joined.

The fighting was fierce, and it was not long before Lachlan Mor, cutting a path for himself through the enemy ranks with his great double-headed axe, found himself face to face with his nephew, the MacDonald Chief. But strangely enough, the thought that this was his own sister's son restrained him. *"A Sheumais! A Sheumais! a mhic mo pheathar!"* he cried, "James, James, son of my sister!" *"fag mo radhad!",* "keep out of my way!" and brought his great axe down, not on his nephew's head, but on that of the MacDonald clansman who stood beside him.

Meanwhile, Dubh Sith, the offer of whose services had been readily accepted by the MacDonalds, had perched himself in the branches of a nearby rowan tree and was biding his time. In the heat of battle, Lachlan Mor lifted the visor of his helmet. This was the moment the dwarf had been waiting for. Taking careful aim, he fired an arrow which pierced Lachlan's left eye and killed him stone dead.

Heavily outnumbered, the Macleans fought on desperately, making their Chief's body a rallying point. Their retreat had been cut off, and no reinforcements could reach them. Fighting to the last, a remnant of the force barricaded themselves into the nearby church, which their enemies then burned down with the Macleans inside it. The clan's motto, *Vel vincere vel mori,* offered a choice of two rewards: victory or death. At *Traigh Ghruinnaird,* the latter was the reward of every one of them.

That night, Lachlan's old nurse, who, as it happened, lived nearby, went down to the battlefield to seek out his body. Then she and her son Duncan loaded it on to a farm cart and set out southwards along the shore of Loch Gorm for Kilchoman, in order to bury it there. The road they took was a rough one, and, with the jolting of the cart, the dead man's head jerked and nodded in a comical manner. Looking round and seeing this, Duncan, who was driving the cart, laughed out loud. It was the last thing he did. Seizing the dead man's dirk, Lachlan's old nurse drove it into the boy's back, and, taking the reins herself, left him dying by the road, happy, for her part, in the knowledge that this insult to Lachlan's memory had not gone unavenged.

Lachlan Mor still lies where she buried him at Kilchoman, beside the church, under a great stone. Duncan they buried by the roadside, where his mother had struck him down, under a pile of stones known to this day as Cairnduncan or Duncan's Cairn.

Macfarlane of Arrochar and the Laird of Luss

"IN THE AGE of the Stewart kings," says the Seanachie, "many of the Highland chiefs had castles of their own for purposes of defence, as well as dwelling houses to suit their convenience." It was thus that, in the days of King James VI, Macfarlane of Arrochar, whose domains straddled the narrow neck of land between Loch Lomond and Loch Long, had a castle on the island of Inveruglas in Loch Lomond and another on *Eilean a'Bhutha*. His dwelling house, on the other hand, was at Cladach Mor, on the shore of the loch near Tarbet. For the residence of a chief, it was not a very large nor very grand house, being thatched with bracken and measuring exactly thirty-four feet long by thirteen feet wide. In it there were just three rooms, a dwelling chamber, a kitchen, with a little pantry between; the kitchen fire was in the middle of the floor, the smoke escaping through a hole in the roof; in the dwelling chamber there was a good-sized window with six panes of glass and there was a smaller glazed window in the kitchen; in the back was a window hole, which was shut with boards when the wind blew. The house was built on one floor. But, says the Seanachie, "beams of cleft oak covered with sods of turf formed a loft above the Laird of Arrochar."

In 1592, Macfarlane of Arrochar's wife was of the ancient and noble family of Buchanan, whose lands lay at the farther end of Loch Lomond. In those days it was quite usual for lairds' wives to spin wool and flax for making cloth. "Macfarlane's lady," says the Seanachie, "was much taken up with spinning and, like the others, did not deem it unbecoming to go herself to the weaver's house with the yarn and give orders to him about weaving it." In this instance, the weaver's house was at some distance farther south, at Banairidh near Ros Dubh on Loch Lomond. Standing on the promontory of *Ros Dubh,* the Black Headland, overlooking the loch, was the splendid residence of Sir Humphrey Colquhoun of Luss, the handsome Chief of Clan Colquhoun, an old friend of Lady Macfarlane's family. In addition to his fine dwelling house Sir Humphrey also possessed a well-fortified stronghold in the lower part of nearby Glen Fruin.

What, then, could have been more natural than that when Macfarlane's wife, a good-looking and headstrong young woman, went to see the weaver she should also sometimes encounter her old friend, Sir Humphrey. As happens in country places, these meetings were noticed and talked about. Macfarlane's lady, it began to be said, was spending a great deal of time in the company of the Laird of Luss. "From which," says the Seanachie, "a scandal arose . . . and Macfarlane's jealousy was excited in consequence."

One summer it so happened that Lady Macfarlane was engaged in spinning more than usually large quantities of yarn to make a great web. This not unnaturally necessitated more than her usual number of visits to the weaver at Banairidh. Noticing her frequent absences, her husband grew even more jealous and did his best to force her to stay at home. At that time, there was no road between Tarbet and Ros Dubh, and Lady Macfarlane was obliged to make the journey by boat. One day, she announced to her husband that she had received a message from the weaver to say that he urgently required some special instructions concerning the web he was weaving for her. Macfarlane asked why she could not send someone else, but she insisted that she must go herself — the instructions were complicated. While she was hurriedly preparing to leave, a letter fell

from her bosom on to the floor. She did not notice this and her husband was able to pick it up and put it in his pocket. After she had gone, he read it. It was from the Laird of Luss at Banairidh, making an assignation for that very day.

This confirmed Macfarlane's worst suspicions, and he at once flew into a towering rage. He had at that time, between Loch Lomond and Loch Long, a large number of men at arms standing by, whom he held in readiness for just such an emergency. Assembling his entire force and putting himself at their head, he now set out for Banairidh, across the hills from Arrochar. Having climbed Inverreoch and reached first Glen Douglas and then Glen Luss, they crossed the River Luss at Cuil a'chipean and then, passing Auchengavin, went through Allt a'chlaidheimh. On reaching the top of Banairidh, the first thing they saw was Macfarlane's lady and Sir Humphrey walking together through the wood.

At the same instant, Macfarlane's lady saw them. "Flee quickly," she cried to Sir Humphrey, "but not to your house. Make for your castle of Bannachra. These men," she added a trifle superfluously, "are for being at you."

"Sir Humphrey," says the Seanachie, "did not wait for another word, but fled. And Macfarlane and his men pursued." Castle Bannachra was five miles away, but although some of Macfarlane's men were very fleet of foot, not one of them caught up with Sir Humphrey, who, leaving Lady Macfarlane to fend for herself, ran faster than any of them. Before the Macfarlanes could overtake him, he had reached his castle and flung himself inside and his retainers with him and barred the great door. By a misfortune, however, one of his serving men was not quite quick enough and was left outside and, being unable to get into the castle, hid himself in an outhouse.

When Macfarlane and his men reached Bannachra, they sought to beat down the great door, but it resisted all their efforts. They next searched the outhouses, and in one of them came on Sir Humphrey's unfortunate serving man, who was at once brought before Macfarlane. The latter's mood, as his wife had rightly surmised, was far from friendly. Drawing his sword, he pointed it at the serving man's chest. "If you do not tell me this moment the place in which Sir Humphrey is," he said, "I will put this sword in through one side of you and out the other."

"The servant's life," says the Seanachie, "was precious to him." Without further ado, he revealed in exactly which part of the castle Sir Humphrey was most likely to be. Thereafter, his unheroic conduct on this occasion was held against him by the people of Luss, and he was popularly known as Traitor Colquhoun, as were his descendants for many generations after him.

Once Macfarlane knew just where Sir Humphrey was lurking, he quickly sent his men into the woods to cut green branches from the trees. These they stacked in a great heap to windward of the castle and then set fire to them. When the wind carried the smoke into the part of the castle where Sir Humphrey was, it almost choked him. Unable to stand the smoke any longer, he sought one of the window holes to breathe the fresh air. "And," says the Seanachie, "one of the Macfarlanes, who was standing opposite the window hole with a bow in his hand, fired an arrow at him and killed him."

Once Macfarlane's men had finally broken into the castle, they dragged out Sir Humphrey's body and cut off his head.

They also cut off his private parts and, wrapping them in a cloth, took them away with them. By the time Macfarlane reached Cladach Mor again, it was time for dinner. Putting Sir Humphrey's private parts on a wooden platter, he placed them in front of his wife. "That," he said, "is your share. You will understand yourself what it is."

*   *   *   *

That Sir Humphrey was slain by an arrow there can be no doubt, but according to another, possibly more reliable source, he was shot, not by a Macfarlane but by his own younger brother, Iain, who, being anxious to supplant him, took this heaven-sent opportunity to get him out of the way. In the event, however, Sir Humphrey was not succeeded by Iain who, soon after Humphrey's death, was carried off to Edinburgh and tried and executed at the Mercat Cross for, of all things, murdering his own brother.

Cnoc an t-Sithein

AT BREIGHIG, or Broad Bay, on the eastern side of the Isle of Barra, there once lived a man who spent much of his time by the shore, searching for anything the waves might have washed up, for in those days shipwrecks were more common than they are now.

Round the headland of Ru Mor, just to the south of Breighig, was a creek called Port an Duine, well known for the number of things that were washed up there. One day, when the wind was blowing from the southeast, a wind particularly favourable for such windfalls, the man was standing above the creek, looking down over the shore. But all he could see lying on the wet sand was a human jawbone with beautiful white teeth. Walking down to the shore, he picked it up and, studying it, said to himself, "This is after being the finest set of teeth I have ever seen." Then he threw it down again.

But as he was walking back up from the shore, suddenly he heard the pipes being played better than he had ever heard them played before. The sound seemed to come from under the ground, in front of him. As he came closer and the music grew louder, he noticed a flat stone set in the sea turf, and, lifting this up, saw a flight of stairs leading downwards. Going down these, he found, says the Seanachie, "the piper, dressed in kilts and playing the pipes—old and grey-headed and beautifully dressed in the green, with silver-buckled shoes." And the piper made the man welcome and invited him to sit by a fire that was burning brightly on the hearth. And the piping continued. Then food was brought to the man, which he much enjoyed. But after only a short time, he was told that he could stay no longer but

must go back up the stairs and, when he came to the top, put the stone back, just as he had found it.

This the man did and, after reaching the top and replacing the stone, set out for home round Ru Mor in the direction of Breighig. But when he came to his home, there was nothing there but bracken and nettles and rushes, no sign of human habitation at all. "And that," says the Seanachie, "is the very wonderful part of the story — all this happening in so short a time." And the man, looking about him, was greatly disturbed and knew that he must have been in *Cnoc an t-Sithein*, the Fairy Knoll. Nor, when he looked about him, could he see any houses save one, a good way away. To this he now made his way.

In the house was a cobbler, a very old man, mending boots. "Come in," said the cobbler. "You are a stranger."

"Yes," said the man, "I am a stranger." And he told him how he had gone round Ru Mor and down to Port an Duine, to the shore.

"And the cobbler," says the Seanachie, "halted and began to ransack his mind." First he said he had never heard of the man, then, after a time, he said, "Yes, I remember. I remember seeing my great-grandfather, and he heard from his father that an old man went round the shore at the Ru Mor and never came back. And so you must be the man I heard of from my great-grandfather now."

And the man who had been in the Fairy Knoll sat down on the cobbler's bench, and all at once he felt himself getting very feeble. And he asked the cobbler to send to the church at Eoligarry that was built in the days of Saint Columba. And a priest came from the church and gave the man the last rites. "And," says the Seanachie, "as soon as that was done — very peculiar — he crumpled down, a lump of earth."

The Skerry of the Blacksmith's Daughter

THERE ONCE DWELT at Strebhnis, on the island of Islay, a man of the name of Macintyre. And in the same parish there lived a woman who was in love with him and who had reason to hope that he would one day marry her. But, when the time came, he did not marry her. Instead, he married the daughter of the blacksmith.

In consequence of this the woman who was in love with Macintyre conceived in her heart a bitter hatred for the woman he had married. But, says the Seanachie, she nevertheless did not in the least show it. On the contrary, she went out of her way to make friends with MacIntyre's wife and to see as much of her as she could.

The years passed by, and one day the two women went down to the shore together to gather shellfish. After they had been gathering shellfish for a while, they felt tired and walked out to a skerry some way from the shore, and there sat down to rest. At low tide there is no water between this skerry and the shore, but at high tide the sea rushes in and covers it and completely fills the channel that surrounds it.

As they were sitting together on the skerry, the woman who was in love with Macintyre brought out a comb and began to comb his wife's abundant tresses so soothingly that, after a time, she fell asleep. Once she was asleep, the other woman, pretending to plait her hair, tied it strand by strand to the seaweed that grew on the skerry. Then, seeing that the tide was coming in fast, she made her way back to the shore and sat down there to watch what happened.

In due course, Macintyre's wife was awakened by the sea washing over her. Realizing her danger, she called out to her companion to come and rescue her. But, with joy in her heart, the other woman now stood up and started to walk away.

"Do you not pity a woman drowning? *Hoog O!*" wailed Macintyre's wife after her.

"I do not pity her in the least," was the reply. "She is no concern of mine. *Heery Horo!*" And left her there to drown.

To this day, the skerry, which can at low tide be discerned without too much difficulty immediately below Strebhnis, is known as the Skerry of the Blacksmith's Daughter.

The Death of Red Colin

FOLLOWING THE RISING of 1745 and the defeat of the
Jacobites at the Battle of Culloden, times, says the Seanachie, were hard in the Highlands. Both rich and poor who had
come out for Prince Charles were plundered. Neither cow nor
horse, sheep nor goat was left to them; the blankets were taken
off their beds and the clothes stripped off their backs; even the
skeins of yarn were taken out of the dye pots, and their houses
were set on fire. In the main, the Jacobites were loyal to each
other, gathering together as one body to try to conceal from King
George's men where the outlaws were hiding and to find means
of sending them food. They shared what they possessed with one
another and concealed their affairs as best they could from those
who were on the king's side. But, as happens in such situations,
there were traitors among them who, when they could, passed
information to the government. "And so," says the Seanachie,
"when a man went to a neighbour's house to speak of any
matter, he would first look around and ask, 'Is the roof of this
house leaking?' If only friends were present, the answer was 'No'.
But if this was not so, the reply was 'Yes. Watch where you sit.'"
Such were the difficulties which afflicted those who remained
loyal to the House of Stewart.

After the Rising, the lands of those who had supported Prince
Charles were confiscated and government factors put in to
manage them and collect the rents. For the lands of Cameron of
Lochiel and Stewart of Appin, Colin Campbell of Glenure was
appointed factor. Glenure was a younger son of Campbell of
Barcaldine and his second wife, the daughter of Cameron of
Lochiel. A red-haired man, he was known in the district as
Cailean Ruadh, or Red Colin. He had served with the Hanoverian

forces in 1745 and 1746, and had earned the reputation of being "very vicious against those who rose with the Prince".

This, it was said, Glenure had shown in no uncertain fashion when, after the Duke of Cumberland's victory at Culloden, the Laird of Kinlochmoidart and the brother of MacDonald of Keppoch were taken prisoner by the government forces. Both had removed their badges of rank and were mingling with the throng of common soldiers in the hope of thus making their way home unrecognized. Seeing them, some government officers who were present and had known them before the Rising gave no sign of recognition. But then Glenure appeared. "Oh!" he said, looking at the prisoners, "Here is the Laird of Kinlochmoidart, who was a major in the army of the Prince. And here is the brother of MacDonald of Keppoch, who was also an officer in Prince Charles's army." Whereupon, the two youths were seized, thrown into jail, and, after a form of trial, condemned to death as traitors. First they were hanged but taken down before they were dead. Then their hearts were cut out and thrown in their faces. After this they were beheaded, their bodies burned, and their ashes scattered to the wind. One story has it that in MacDonald two hearts were found.

In the years that followed, Colin of Glenure missed no chance of harassing the Jacobites, taking special care to make no exception for his mother's clan, the Camerons. "I will be upsides with these men," he said. "I will see to it that not a clod of land in Appin stays in Stewart hands and not a clod of land in Lochaber in Cameron hands." "This language," says the Seanachie, "excited great anger and hatred in the people of Appin and Lochaber against Colin of Glenure."

Whenever the opportunity offered, Glenure suited his actions to his words, hunting down fugitives remorselessly and himself summarily despatching a woman who had bravely sought to save her son-in-law's life by throwing herself in front of him, crying, "Colin! Colin! Let him go with his life!" But Glenure had pressed the trigger notwithstanding, and shot her dead. "Such deeds as these," says the Seanachie, "excited great hatred against Colin in those who were friendly to the people who rose with the Prince. And they wished Colin dead."

Charles Stewart of Ardsheil, who had fought for Prince Charles, was by now in exile in France; his lands had been confiscated, and *Seumas a'Ghlinne*, James of the Glen, his father's natural son, paid rent for them to Glenure as tenant. The rent he paid was a low one, and James passed on a part of the income from the land to his half-brother's wife, Isobel. But Glenure, on learning of this from an informer, at once confiscated all James's cattle and provisions and, evicting him from Ardsheil, let the estate on a long lease to a fellow Campbell. "This," says the Seanachie, "caused great loss to James of the Glen . . . He thenceforth became much addicted to drink and, when he would be drunk, as often he was, he reviled Colin of Glenure, spoke of his ill will to him, threatened that he should do as much harm to Colin as Colin had done to him. And he did not conceal his resentment." As for the Lady of Ardsheil, she was obliged to leave Appin with her children and seek refuge elsewhere, before joining her husband in France.

Meanwhile, Colin of Glenure continued to show no indulgence to the people of Appin and Lochaber, and, when these sent two gentlemen of the country to reason with him, he simply repeated what he had already said, namely that he would not cease from what he was doing so long as a single clod of land remained in Stewart or Cameron hands. "This language," says the Seanachie, "spread through the whole of Appin and Lochaber. If he continued to do as he was doing, it was said, it would not be long before none of the old inhabitants would be left in the country. There had been hatred against Colin before, and the people would most sincerely have been glad to see him dead. But, when they heard his language anew, the wish came to them to kill him themselves." It was a wish that was widely shared.

A first plan to give effect to this wish was hatched by the Laird of Callart, who volunteered to put a bullet through Colin while he was taking his usual evening stroll. Callart abandoned the plan, however, following a private talk over supper with Stewart of Fasnacloich. A new proposal was now put forward. It was decided that some of the principal men of Appin should meet together at Glenstockdale in Appin. The scene is best described in the words of the Seanachie: "There were," he says, "some men in the country who had not given up their arms to the King, and were among the most esteemed in the country. Every man who had a gun was to bring his gun with him, in order that its goodness might be tested. The place they chose for trying the guns was a place called Lag Bhlair an Lochain, where the sound of the guns fired would not be heard far off.

"There were three guns in Appin and Glencoe at that time. John Stewart, who dwelt at Caolas nan Con, had a gun, and the name he had for it was *a'Chuilbhearnach*. It was a Spanish gun, a very good one of its kind. The Laird of Fasnacloich had a two-barrelled gun. There was another man in Appin, of the name of Dugald MacColl, by some called Dugald of the Whisker, who had a big, long Spanish gun, and his name for it was *an t-Slinneanach*. It was an excellent gun for casting bullets. They met on the day which they had appointed, at the place where they were to meet, but, before they began firing, they swore to each other that they would keep the affair about which they were going secret; and that those who had the guns were to give them up to those who were the best shots. The best shot was to get the best gun and do the special hunting. They tried the guns, and Dugald MacColl's gun, the *Slinneanach* or Broad-shouldered One, was the best. It would put a bullet and a swan-shot within two inches of each other near the middle of the target at the distance of a hundred yards. A man called Donald Stewart, a

136

nephew of the Laird of Ballachulish, was the best hand at the gun. He could put the ball and swan-shot in the middle of the mark with the *Slinneanach*. Dugald MacColl delivered the *Slinneanach* to him, and Donald was chosen as the man for the shooting of Glenure. The Laird of Fasnacloich was the second-best shot; he was chosen to be Donald Stewart's comrade."

Not long after this came the news that it was Colin of Glenure's intention to go to Lochaber on business connected with the Cameron lands there. With him he was taking his nephew Mungo Campbell, his brother Barcaldine's natural son, whom he had decided to make factor for the lands of Lochiel in his place, being by this time, for reasons that can be imagined, afraid to go there himself. The conspirators accordingly now decided to take advantage of this journey of Colin's to lie in wait for him and kill him on his way back. With this purpose in view, the Camerons were to keep watch for him in Lochaber. Farther along the route would lurk Big Donald Og MacMartin of Dochanassy in the hope that he might get a shot at Red Colin. The Lairds of Onich and Callart would wait at Onich. Finally, on the other side of Loch Leven, Donald Stewart, nephew of the Laird of Ballachulish, would take up his position with Stewart of Fasnacloich by a big black rock between Ballachulish and Lettermore. There they were to lie in wait in the wood, with *Slinneanach* and Fasnacloich's gun resting on the branch of a big birch tree.

On Saturday 14th May 1752, Glenure, having completed his business in Lochaber, set out for home, accompanied by his nephew Mungo and John Mackenzie, his gillie. When Glenure reached the place where Big Donald Og of Dochanassy was to be lying in wait for him, Big Donald was not there. He had started too late and did not arrive on the scene until after Colin and his companions had passed. On discovering this, Donald flew into a rage. "How have you let Colin of Glenure pass?" he enquired furiously of his companion, who was supposed to be keeping watch.

"I was asleep when he came," the man replied sheepishly, "and he passed unknown to me." Whereupon, Big Donald, whose dignity had suffered, bustled off after Colin in the direction of Onich, where the Lairds of Onich and Callart were waiting.

By now Red Colin's gillie, John Mackenzie, who was himself from Onich, had learned that there were men waiting along the road for his master with guns, and was bravely keeping as close to him as he could. It thus happened that, when Colin reached Onich, Mackenzie was riding in the direct line of fire between him and the Lairds of Onich and Callart, who were lying in wait for him, but were afraid to shoot at him for fear of killing Mackenzie, whose father they knew. "For this reason," says the Seanachie, "Colin got past Onich, as he did past the other place previously."

Not long after Colin had passed through Onich, Big Donald Og came galloping up in a state of high indignation. "How have you let the rogue pass without giving him his desert?" he asked angrily of the Lairds of Callart and Onich.

"The gillie Mackenzie," they replied, "was between us and him, and we did not get firing at him as we were afraid we might kill Mackenzie with him."

This made Big Donald Og even angrier. "Had I been there when he passed," he declared, "I should have fired the shot, even if it meant killing Mackenzie also. I am sure the men on the other side will not be so slack as those on this side have been. I will not leave this place until I hear the sound of the firing." And he sat down to listen with keen anticipation for the sound of shots from the other side of the loch.

When Glenure and his companions reached the ferry at Ballachulish, known as Caolas Mhic Pharuig, they found *Postair Cam,* the One-eyed Ferryman, by name Archibald MacInnes, awaiting them. It was said by some that, though one-eyed, Archie was gifted with second sight and knew of things that were to happen before they came to pass. Be that as it may, he knew full well that there were people along the way who were ill disposed to Red Colin and were seeking an opportunity to eliminate him. "Colin," he said to him, "if you will take my advice you will not at all go down the side of Loch Leven tonight, but go home through Gleann an Fhiudharich, so that no harm may happen to you."

"I will not do that," replied Colin. "But I will go down the way

of Ardsheil — I have business there, and I will go that way."

"Well," said the One-eyed Ferryman, "my advice to you is to take a boat and go down the middle of the loch, and to keep as far from the land as you can so that a ball may not reach you."

"I am not in the least afraid of that," said Colin. "Assuredly, I was afraid in Lochaber. I had enough fear of my mother's clan. But now, since I have got whole from the country of my mother, I am not the least afraid."

And so the One-eyed Ferryman put Colin and Mungo and Mackenzie the gillie and their horses across the ferry, and when they reached the other side they mounted their horses and jogged off along the road to Lettermore. They had not gone far when they encountered Iain Stewart of Ballachulish, or *Iain Buidhe,* Yellow-haired Iain, as he was known. "It is better for you to stay in my house tonight, Colin," said Ballachulish, whose nephew Donald was, as he almost certainly knew, lying in wait for Colin with the *Slinneanach* a short distance farther on. "Better to take a night's hospitality with me and go away in the morning."

But Red Colin, having thanked him, replied, "I will not stay. I am in a hurry to go to Ardsheil, and I am desirous of being forward as soon as I can."

"You are welcome," said the Laird of Ballachulish, "to stay a night with me if you like, and I do think it were better for you to stay."

"It is going forward that I will do," replied Colin. "I have business to settle in Ardsheil."

And so Colin of Glenure and his nephew Mungo rode on ahead, and Stewart of Ballachulish and Mackenzie the gillie, following more slowly, soon lost sight of them. And when Glenure and Mungo reached the black rock near Lettermore, where the Laird of Fasnacloich and Ballachulish's nephew Donald Stewart were hiding, a shot was fired, and two balls struck Colin in his left side, between his ribs and his armpit. At this, his horse reared up, and he fell sideways in the saddle, crying, "Oh Mungo, Mungo! Flee! Flee as fast as the legs of your horse will carry you. I am shot." After which his horse blundered into a gate by the side of the track, and he, hanging sideways from the saddle, hit the gatepost and, falling to the ground, never spoke again.

From where they were, Stewart of Ballachulish and Mackenzie the gillie heard the shot. "That shot," said Ballachulish to Mackenzie, "has done harm. I hope Colin of Glenure is safe and that he went down by the shore." Then he turned back towards Ballachulish, while Mackenzie hurried on to see what had happened to his master.

At Onich, across the loch, they also heard the shot. Ponderously, Big Donald Og MacMartin of Dochanassy rose to his feet. "My business is done now," he said complacently to those who were with him. "I may go home. I knew the gallant men on the other side would not let that rogue pass them in such a silly manner as those on this side did."

When Mackenzie reached the place where his master had been shot, Glenure was lying dead in his blood by the side of the path, with Mungo his nephew standing beside him. As soon as Mackenzie came in sight, Mungo called out to him, "Go as fast as you can to the house of James of the Glen and try to get him and any others who may be there to come and lift Colin of Glenure." And Mackenzie, horrorstruck, put spurs to his horse and rode as hard as he could go to James's house.

James of the Glen, who now lived nearby at Aucharn, had been sowing barley that day. The ground had been soft, and James was dirty, with clay over the knees. Hearing a horseman approaching, "I do not like the sound of that horse," he said. "It is ridden too hard." James was standing warming himself, with his back to the fire, when Mackenzie knocked at the door. Hearing the knocking, he left the fire and, as the door was opened, went into his bedchamber. Mackenzie caught sight of him as he entered the house, but gave no sign of this. On asking whether the good man was in, he was told that he was not. Then Mackenzie blurted out that his master had been killed between Ballachulish and Lettermore. When James had put on clean clothes, he came back into the room, and Mackenzie repeated his story.

"Co'sam bith an ciontach, is mise an creineach," said James, "Whoever is guilty, it is I who will pay the penalty." Mackenzie then asked James to come back with him and lift Colin of Glenure. This James himself was willing to do, but his wife was against it, and in the end he did not go.

Meanwhile, as dusk was falling and young Mungo Campbell was waiting by his uncle's body and trying to quench the flow of blood, a woman came by, wearing a handkerchief over her shoulders. "Were you to be so good, woman, as to give me your handkerchief," Mungo said to her, "I would pay you for it."

"I will not, indeed," replied the woman. "It is in the shop that I bought my handkerchief. Go you to the shop and buy a handkerchief as I did."

"There is a man here," said Mungo, "who has been killed by a shot which someone has fired at him, and it is for quenching the blood that I ask for the handkerchief."

"Let the hunter now drink the soup," said the woman sharply and went on her way.

Thinking over the incident afterwards, Mungo wondered if this had been an ordinary woman. There had been something strange about her, yet she had looked somehow familiar, like, it suddenly occurred to him, the woman Colin had once shot dead as she was seeking to protect her son-in-law.

Once Mackenzie the gillie had gathered the men he needed, he came back with them to where his master's body lay. Together they took the body by boat to the house of the miller at Kintallen nearby, put it in a barn and let it lie there till a bier had been made for it, after which the body was taken away and eventually buried at Ardchattan Priory, in the ancient burial place of the Campbells of Barcaldine.

When Glenure's kinsmen and the other gentlemen of Clan Campbell heard of the murder, they were, not unnaturally, much enraged. "And," says the Seanachie, "they were ransacking through the country, trying if they could find out those who had ill will to him." It was now recalled that, after Glenure had turned James of the Glen out of Ardsheil and taken all his cattle and provisions, James, when drunk, as he now often was, had repeatedly cursed him for the harm he had done him and said that, if he had the chance, he would do as much harm to Colin as Colin had done to him. Indeed, once, when James had been with some people at an inn and one of them had, perhaps a little provocatively, proposed the health of Colin of Glenure, James had replied, "I will not myself drink the health of Colin of Glenure." "What would you do then?" had rejoined the other. "Were he on the gallows," had said James, "I would draw down his feet." "And," says the Seanachie, "there was notice taken of this remark, and it was kept in remembrance. And when a large reward was offered to any person who should give information of those who had ill will to Colin, there was information given of the language which James of the Glen had spoken, and he was seized and sent to jail."

Information was likewise sent to the Sheriff of Inveraray that, on the day when Colin of Glenure was killed, Stewart of Fasnacloich had been seen going to the moor, armed. Accordingly, Fasnacloich was seized and brought to court. It was also said that some time previously Fasnacloich had sent a serving man to his kinsman, William Stewart, usually known as *Uileam Mor Mac-Donnachaich Fhuiden*, to fetch a small packet. When Fasnacloich opened the packet, the serving man had seen that it contained some lead bullets and a mould for making them, which bore the number of a gun. But when Fasnacloich was taken to Inveraray, the serving man fled out of the country and did not return for three or four years. "It is not known," says the Seanachie, "what evidence that serving man might have brought against Fasnacloich had he been found — but he was not found."

One witness called against Fasnacloich was Donald Macintyre, known as Domnhall Ban, a gillie in the service of Stewart of Invernahyle. Like Fasnacloich, Donald had been out with the Prince. Asked on oath by the sheriff whether he had seen the Laird of Fasnacloich going in arms to the moor on the day Colin of Glenure was killed, he replied "No". There were no other witnesses on that point, and so the case was dropped and Fasnacloich set free.

Some time after this, Fasnacloich saw Domnhall Ban at work in a field. "Come here, Domnhall Ban," he said, "I want a word with you." At this, Domnhall Ban came over to him. "I am much obliged to you, Domnhall Ban," said Fasnacloich, "for having perjured yourself to save me at Inveraray."

"Oh devil's spawn," rejoined Domnhall Ban good-humouredly, "and would you be saying that I perjured myself for you?"

"Well then, tell me," said Fasnacloich, "how do you clear yourself?"

"The sheriff asked me," said Donald, "'Did you see the Laird of Fasnacloich in arms on the day on which Colin of Glenure was killed?' I said 'No', for you had but a gun, and one gun is not arms; it is but an arm."

"Right enough," said Fasnacloich, and they shook hands.

"There were not," says the Seanachie, "many of the gentlemen or others who were somewhat respected that rose with Prince Charles, either in Lochaber or in Appin of MacIain Stiubhart, who were not some way connected with the plot against the life of Colin of Glenure. They were now under the fear that there should be a ransacking out about it and that there should be information of their connection with it obtained. So they devised a plan to put those who were in search of evidence off the scent."

The plan these gentlemen devised concerned a certain Allan Stewart, a foster son of James of the Glen, usually called Allan Breck or Speckled Allan, his face being deeply pitted with the smallpox. An adventurous character who had fought on both sides in the Forty-five and was eventually to become an officer in the French army, he had been in Appin when Colin was killed. In return for a reward, Allan Breck now agreed to take to the hills for a time and let it be put about that he was the murderer, "for the purpose", as the Seanachie puts it, "of lessening enquiries concerning the rest of the gentlemen and sending those who sought for the guilty to search the country for him. And the people of the country were all faithful to him for, while he was not taken, he was concealing the guilt of those who did the ill deed."

After skulking for a time in the hills, Allan Breck finally found means of going to France, whence he sent back a letter declaring that he was the man who had killed Colin of Glenure. "But the letter," says the Seanachie, "did not reach soon enough to be of use to James of the Glen."

On 21st September 1752, James of the Glen was brought to trial in the old courthouse at Inveraray on a charge of complicity in the murder of Colin of Glenure. Like other trials before and since, his trial was largely intended as a warning to others and its issue a foregone conclusion.

The presiding judge was Archibald Campbell, Third Duke of Argyll and Lord Justice General of Scotland. Of the fifteen jurymen, eleven bore the name of Campbell. Among the prosecuting counsel was Simon Fraser, once Master of Lovat and now lately called to the Scottish Bar, whose knowledge of Gaelic was a convenience, and who, following his father's execution for high treason and his own participation in the Rising, was painfully anxious to conciliate the government and make a new life for himself.

James's trial, says the Seanachie, lasted three days "without anything being found against him that would make him guilty." On the third day, a certain John Breck MacColl from Glenduror was called as a witness against him. John MacColl was an orphan whom James had befriended and brought up in his own house. He had spent much time with James in the inn and had often heard him abusing Colin of Glenure. But nothing in his evidence was of sufficient consequence to enable even that court to condemn James. On coming out of the courthouse, however, John MacColl met his wife, and the two of them talked of the evidence John had given.

"Did you tell them," asked his wife, "that you heard James of the Glen once say, when he was drunk, that he would go a mile on his knees to make a blackcock of Colin?"

"Indeed, I did not remember that," replied John.

"Well," said his wife, "you had better go back in and tell it to them."

"I do not like to return to the courthouse again, since I did not remember it when I was in," replied John, but in the end his wife persuaded him, and he went back and said to the court, "I forgot something when I was in before, gentlemen. There is a little thing I did not remember to tell you."

"Come on, then," they replied, "and enter the witness box and let us hear what you have to say."

And John MacColl again entered the witness box and said, "Once, when he was drunk, I heard the prisoner, James Stewart, say that he would go three miles on his knees on the ice to make a blackcock of Colin of Glenure." And as soon as the judge heard this, he passed sentence, declaring that James Stewart was to be hanged on a gallows on the mound of Cnap a'Chaolais at Balla-chulish; that his body was to be left hanging until it fell down; and that his bones were to be put up again and left hanging on the gallows until they decayed.

When Donald Stewart, the nephew of the Laird of Ballachul-ish, heard that James of the Glen was in prison under sentence of death, he was much distressed by the thought that an innocent man was to be hanged for a crime he had not committed, and seriously considered giving himself up to be hanged in his place. But when his friends heard that he was intending to do this, they were deeply disturbed at the thought that he might by his action involve them all. And so they did everything possible to dissuade him, representing to him that it was far better that one innocent man should be put to death than that a common destruction should be brought on all the people of the country, and that even if he, Donald, were to give himself up, it would not save James from the gallows but simply mean that both of them would be hanged. Indeed, there was grave danger that all connected with the plot would be discovered, and that those who were not slaughtered would be exiled from the kingdom. In the end, they managed with great difficulty to persuade him. But Donald fell sick with grief-fever and took to his bed and, says the Seanachie, "lay in it for a long time thereafter".

And so in due course a gallows was erected at Cnap a'Chaolais, by Ballachulish Ferry, and on 8th November 1752 James of the Glen was hanged on it. Some Camerons, it is said, made a plan to rescue him on his way to the gallows, but James dissuaded them. It would, he said, do more harm to his country than his life was worth.

Before being hanged, James asked one of the two ministers present to read him the Thirty-fifth Psalm, and in Appin and Lochaber this psalm was long known as *Salm Sheaumais a' Ghlinne,* the Psalm of James of the Glen: "For without cause have they hid for me their net in a pit, which without cause they digged for my soul . . . False witnesses did rise up; they laid to my charge things that I knew not."

After he had been hanged, James's body was left hanging in chains on the gallows, as directed by the court. "And this," says the Seanachie, "was very trying to his friends, for the gallows were in sight of his widow's house and of those of his two married sisters and of the house, too, of the Laird of Ballachulish. And there was not a time that they looked towards Ardsheil that they did not see James hanging there."

Some time after this, when Stewart of Ballachulish's nephew Donald had recovered from his fever, he and Colin of Glenure's brother Alexander Campbell, son of the Laird of Barcaldine, went with their dogs and their gillies to Rannoch Moor to hunt deer. With him, Donald took his long gun, the *Slinneanach.* After walking all day without seeing a stag, they sat down towards evening in a hollow to eat the food they had brought with them. And while they were eating, they suddenly saw on the skyline what seemed to be a stag's antlers. "Whistle," said Donald to his gillie, but nothing moved. "Whistle louder," said Donald, and the gillie whistled louder. This time a stag stood up. Donald rested his long gun and took aim.

"You fool," said Alexander. "Do you think you can hit it at that distance?" Donald fired, and the stag fell. "You have done it," said Alexander. "I did not think that any gun could do it at that distance."

Together they went to where the stag lay and looked at where he had been hit. The holes made by the two shots fired from the gun were about twice the breadth of each hole from one another and were situated halfway between the back of the shoulder and the short rib.

"That," said Alexander, looking at the holes, "is the very manner in which Colin my brother was hit, and unless I am much deceived, that is the same gun that did the deed."

"Do you think," asked Donald with unusual directness, "that it was I who killed your brother?"

"I do not say in whose hand the gun was," said Alexander, "but I am much deceived if that is not the gun with which the killing was done."

"Were I to think," replied Donald, "that you imagined that it was I who killed your brother, you should not go home living on your own feet."

"I do not say that it was you who killed my brother," said Alexander Campbell, "but I remark that the gun which you have has put the two balls at the same distance from one another as those which were put in my brother and in much the same manner."

"If I thought you were suspecting me of having killed your brother," said Donald, "you should not go home to say that to another."

"Oh, I do not suspect you," said Alexander. "I do but say that the shots were like each other."

This talk, says the Seanachie, produced a coldness between the two. When they separated, each took a different road home, and thereafter they did not go after deer together.

In due course, Donald Stewart went to sea and did not return to Ballachulish until he was an old man. He died, it is said, in a sheiling in Gleann na n-Iola, and many gentlemen of the country were with him in the hut on the night he died. But then they suddenly took fear and fled out, and did not go in again until it was light, and when they went in they found Donald dead.

The bones of James of the Glen remained hanging in chains from the gallows on Cnap a'Chaolais for some years, as a warning to any Jacobite sympathisers who might pass that way. For a year or two, until finally withdrawn, an armed guard of fifteen soldiers watched the gallows night and day.

In 1761, Duke Archibald of Argyll died and was succeeded by his cousin, General John Campbell of Mamore, a more humane man with great regard for his fellow Highlanders. To Duke John, after some preparatory manoeuvring, came Iain Stewart of Ballachulish with a request for permission to put away the gallows, "his female neighbour" as he called it (for in Gaelic *croich*, the word for "gallows", is feminine), and give what was left of James a decent burial.

"Do not let on anything," replied the Duke in a friendly manner, "but put it away. It was not in accordance with my wish that it was ever there. I did all I could against its being placed there at all, but he who was then Duke of Argyll did as he liked. So put your neighbour away quietly, and I promise you I shall not say a word about it. I feel affronted by the case. In my view it were better that it had not happened."

Today, a granite monument marks the place where the gallows once stood, proclaiming to all and sundry the innocence of Seumas a' Ghlinne, who now lies buried nearby in the ruined kirk at Keil.

Many years later, while tending cattle in the glen behind Ballachulish House, a serving maid called Janet discovered a rusty gun hidden in a hollow tree. She took it to Stewart of Ballachulish, by now a very old man. *"Se sin gunna dubh a' mhi-fhortain, a Sheonaid,"* he said. "That, Janet, is the black gun of misfortune."

As a final comment, I was told by my friend Sir Dugald Stewart of Appin that the name of the man who shot Colin Campbell of Glenure has been secretly handed down from father to son in his family ever since. I did not press him further, preferring to leave my readers to draw their own conclusions.

A Substitution

FACING EACH OTHER OBLIQUELY across a mile or
two of choppy water at the head of Loch Fyne, there stood
some centuries ago two famous castles: on the eastern shore, the
great Campbell fortress of Ardkinglas, with its massive walls and
three great towers (now replaced by a scarcely less massive mod-
ern structure); and, on a little promontory on the western shore,
Dundaramn or Dunderave, the smaller but no less well-fortified
stronghold of MacNeachain an Duin, MacNaughtan of the
Mound, Chief of Clan MacNaughtan, which, skilfully restored
to its original state, still stands there today.

At the time of which we speak, namely in the 18th century, Sir
James Campbell of Ardkinglas was blessed with one son and no
less than eight daughters, all, says the Seanachie, rather sweep-
ingly, as fair as the driven snow, as graceful as the swan, and as
free as the deer on the hill, but not, it appears, all equally beautiful, or, for that matter, possessed of identical characters. Of the
eight daughters, the two eldest were, as it happened, both in love
with their neighbour from across the loch, John MacNaughtan
of the Mound. But John, for his part, greatly preferred Margaret,
the younger of the two sisters, to Jane, the elder and, be it said,
much the plainer. It was Margaret he was in love with, and Margaret he intended to marry. And little wonder, for, in the words
of the Seanachie, "the young lady was exceedingly beautiful and
extremely handsome. So singularly fascinating were her fairness
of face and elegance of form that no eye gazed upon her without
seeking to gaze upon her again." As for John MacNaughtan, it
was his firm intention to gaze upon her day in and day out for the
rest of his life.

149

In those days it was considered, or so people said, unlucky for any but the eldest sister of a family to marry first. Accordingly, every effort was made to dissuade John from his purpose. Why could he not be sensible and marry Jane, they asked. Though she might not be quite as pretty as Margaret, she had, they assured him, a much nicer nature. But John stuck to his guns, and in the end Campbell of Ardkinglas reluctantly agreed to allow Margaret to marry John, though, having grudgingly taken the decision, he at once secretly began to seek a means of reversing it. Nevertheless, in due course the marriage was solemnized, and at Ardkinglas the wine flowed freely, and the feasting lasted far into the night.

Next day, few of the participants had more than a hazy recollection of what had taken place the night before. They could, with an effort, recall the actual wedding ceremony and the bride, heavily veiled, being led up the aisle by her father. They could remember the start of the junketing and how Ardkinglas and his kinsmen had from the start plied the bridegroom unmercifully with liquor. But their memories of what, if anything, had followed were a blank. Of more concern to most of them was the present delicate state of their health.

When John MacNaughtan woke next morning in his own great bedchamber at Dunderave, he was, like his fellow guests, feeling far from well. Gradually, as he lay there, memories of the day before started to come back to him. He had been married. That much was certain. And to Margaret. He clearly remembered the objections her father had raised and how in the end he had overcome them. He could remember her solemn progress up the aisle on old Ardkinglas' sturdy arm. And the heavy veil she had worn. Together, he and she had somehow, he supposed, been conveyed back across the loch to Dunderave. But then why was it, he suddenly asked himself, looking around him, that the head beside his on the pillow and the body beside his in the great canopied bedstead belonged not to Margaret, but to her elder sister Jane?

It was a problem he would sooner not have faced in his present condition, with that intolerable hammering in his head, but one that would inevitably have to be faced and, what is more, faced sooner rather than later. All the more so in view of what had happened since he and his bride, if bride she were, had entered their bridal chamber a good many hours before. Assuming, as he had to assume, that she had been a virgin when he married her, if indeed he had married her, she was certainly not a virgin now. And virginity in those far-away days was a precious asset, not to be lightly trifled with, more especially the virginity of a daughter of so near and powerful a neighbour as Campbell of Ardkinglas, himself a favoured henchman of MacNaughtan's even nearer and far more formidable neighbour, MacCailein Mor, Chief of mighty Clan Campbell.

How, he asked himself hazily, had the mistake occurred, if indeed it was a mistake, which he was beginning to doubt. Had it in fact been Margaret whom her father had led up the aisle under that heavy veil? Or Jane? No less important, had it been Jane or Margaret he had slept with and, it seemed to him, made love to with all the energy at his disposal. Surely, he told himself, he would have been able to tell the difference. But then, as some of his more cynical and coarse-fibred friends kept telling him, in the dark, in bed, one woman was very like another, especially if you had had a certain amount to drink.

Somewhat to his dismay, the latter question was quickly answered. It was Jane who, seeing him stir uneasily, threw her arms around him. "My beloved," she murmured languorously and with an abandon which left him in little doubt of what had passed between them. With the help of that heavy veil, the substitution, he decided, could well have been effected even before the marriage ceremony, but whether then or later that night made little odds. To his own serving-men and women, who were at this very moment waiting outside the door to welcome the bridal pair; to his MacNaughtan clansmen; to the villagers of nearby Inveraray; to his neighbours on both sides of stormy Loch Fyne, including, he recalled with a shudder, his newly acquired father-in-law and that worthy's powerful and illustrious Chief down the road, the bride with whom, when he felt well enough, he would emerge from the bridal chamber would be his wife for better or for worse, till death did them part. And for him to declare that he had been the victim of a deception, that the minister who had married them had probably been part of the plot, that he had been married to the wrong girl under false pretences, would not only do no good, but would make him a laughing stock for the rest of his life, which, he rather ruefully reflected, he in all conscience already was.

And so, with the good nature and good sense for which he was rightly renowned, John MacNaughtan of the Mound, rolling over in bed, returned Jane's embraces in as friendly a manner as he could, and later that morning emerged with her on his arm from the great door of the castle to the plaudits of the assembled populace. It was, he had decided, the decent thing to do, and, like the great majority of us, he prided himself on being decent. Besides which, there was nothing much else he could do. Or so it seemed at the time. . . .

*   *   *   *

For a year or two everything went well. John MacNaughtan continued to fulfil his chiefly duties while the new Lady of Dunderave quickly acquainted herself with those of a chief's wife, performing them with efficiency and zeal. "Though not possessed of a beautiful face," says the Seanachie, "nor of a stately form, his wife was endowed with a nobility of mind, benevolence of heart, and deftness of hand that endeared her to all. The two were happy together in their surroundings."

Their surroundings left nothing to be desired. Dunderave was, and still is, as beautiful a place as you will find in the Western Highlands. Of nowhere could it be more justly said, "this castle has a pleasant seat." The young couple's friends, and they had many, were delighted to be invited there. "There was," says the Seanachie, "much enjoyment at Dunderave. Many friends were there, and various entertainments were given. Man contested with man in strength of arm, in dexterity of hand, and in litheness of limb, while ballad, song and story were told by old and young. During the day brave men hunted the stately stag on the mountainside and the bounding roe in the copse-wood glen, and at night fair women sang their songs of love to the voice of responsive harps, while in their dreams fleet-footed hounds chased again the deer."

Among their regular guests, not unnaturally, was Jane's younger sister, Margaret, now more disturbingly lovely than ever. Although she never spoke of the bitter disappointment she had suffered in being snatched, as it were, from her affianced's arms, her secret sorrow gave her beauty a new, an ethereal quality it had not possessed before. As for John, he felt bound, no less naturally, to be civil to his new sister-in-law. While his guests were pursuing the stately stag on the hill or the bounding roe in the copse-wood glen, while the fair women were singing their love songs before a select and appreciative audience, while Jane was busying herself about the castle as a good housewife should, John and the lovely Margaret were never far apart. For them the copse-wood glen, once the hunters had abandoned the chase, became a favourite meeting place – trysting place, one might soon have said, for now that fate, with a little help from them both, had thrown them together again, they soon found that the old magic was once more at work.

Margaret's nature, we are repeatedly told, had at the best of times never been as nice as her sister's was reputed to be. Her recent experience had done nothing to soften or improve it; on the contrary, it had sharpened it and given it a cutting edge.

Unashamedly, she made hay while the sun shone. Propinquity helped, and, in the words of the Seanachie, "a guilty love grew up between them".

But just how guilty was it, they wondered. John had, as we have seen, always prided himself on trying to do the right, the decent thing. The question he now asked himself was what, in his present difficult circumstances, was the right thing? It was true that he was married to Jane, but through no fault of his. Had he and Margaret not been the victims of a most unpleasant plot, in which Jane herself had played her part? Neither of them, he reckoned, any longer owed any debt to society. Jane, it was true, had great nobility of mind, which he sometimes could not help wishing she would keep to herself. She was, in her limited way, a nice enough creature, though he could not help remembering she had lent herself readily enough to her father's dastardly stratagem. But Margaret aroused in him feelings of an altogether different nature, urges which, now that they could be satisfied, he had no intention of seeking to resist. He and she, he was now more than ever convinced, were made for one another.

It was thus that one fine Monday morning Jane and the other inhabitants of Dunderave awoke to the fact that their Chief was no longer with them. He and Margaret, says the Seanachie "had fled together from the place, never again to return to beloved Dundaramn of the scarlet banners, on the beautiful banks of Loch Fyne." Just what became of them thereafter the Seanachie does not relate, although there is a story, from a second, but no less reliable source, that, having boarded their *birlinn*, the lovers simply sailed on southwards down Loch Fyne and across the sea to Northern Ireland, where they made their home in a place which they named Dunderave after distant Dunderave of the Scarlet Banners and where they lived happily ever after, free to pursue their guilty (or not so guilty) passion undisturbed.*

Jane was less lucky. "The forsaken wife," the Seanachie continues, "was sorely stricken. Her golden hair turned ashen grey, her sparkling eye and youthful form became those of dreary

---

* The MacNaughtans of Dunderave in Co. Antrim seem in fact to have moved there considerably earlier.

age." From her sorrow she sought such relief as she could in songs of her own composing. These had a distinctly vindictive flavour.

> "O woman, who took my husband from me," she sang,
> "May there be sharp thorns under the soles of thy feet
> And may the earth open beneath thee.
> May thy roof leak and cold water ever drip upon thy bedstead."†

But John, as it happened, had left Jane with something to remember him by. Not long after his departure, she found that she was pregnant and in due course was delivered of a fine boy. From the first, old Ardkinglas seemed keenly interested in his grandson and, once the boy was old enough, would often take him out fishing in a boat. But one evening old Ardkinglas came back to the castle alone. Young MacNaughtan, he said, with a great show of distress, had by a mischance fallen overboard and

† This particular song, says Lord Archibald Campbell, he once heard sung "to a weird old air", while another authority states that "it was a favourite song with dairy-maids, when milking", adding that "it seemed to charm the cow to part with the milk to the milker".

been drowned. Not long after this he himself took possession of Dunderave and all the MacNaughtan lands, they being, he explained, the property of an absconding adulterer with no one left to succeed him. And so fair Dunderave of the Scarlet Banners passed into Campbell hands and was soon after incorporated in the estate of Ardkinglas. "And to this day," says the second and, I suspect, more reliable seanachie, "the people of Cairndow can point out the spot where the boy fell in the water."

It was not until some time after all this had happened that the local people recalled that at Margaret's birth an aged Campbell seer had gleefully prophesied that this innocent infant would in her lifetime bring worse disaster on Clan MacNaughtan than a thousand armed enemies.

In a Sieve They went to Sea

IN THE VILLAGE of Slapin on Loch Slapin on the Isle of Skye, there lived a fisherman and a tailor, and they were great neighbours, and their wives were well known to be witches.

One day, says the Seanachie, Donald the fisherman, who had been out all day fishing, came home in the evening very, very tired, and lay down on the bench and fell asleep. And while he was asleep, the tailor's wife came round to visit her neighbour, and the two got talking. And their talk was of where they would go fishing that night. And after a bit, while they were talking, Donald woke up and, without opening his eyes, began to listen to what the two women were saying. When he heard that they were going fishing, he was amused and keen to hear how they would set about it. And as he listened, he heard his wife ask the tailor's wife, "What will we take with us?" And the tailor's wife replied, "We will take the sieve with us." And they went to fetch a sieve.

Once the two had everything in readiness and were about to set out, Donald, who all this time had been lying on the bench seemingly asleep, sat up, stretched himself, so that they could see he was now awake, and asked where they were going. And they told him they were going fishing, adding, "You had better lie down and sleep till we come back."

"Ach," said Donald, who was interested by their talk of going fishing in a sieve and thought it must be a name they had for his new boat, "I had better go with you."

But they utterly refused to take him with them. However, he went with them as far as the shore. And when they arrived on the beach, before they went out, they made him promise that

157

whatever might happen while they were out fishing, he would not say a word, but, most of all, would not, under any circumstances, use the name of God. And Donald promised. "Anything you tell me," he said, by now thoroughly intrigued, "I will agree to it." And the two women took the sieve. "And you will also tell us when we have plenty of herring ashore?" they said. And Donald said, "Yes, that I will do."

"And as they embarked in the sieve," says the Seanachie, "they became two rats. And they moved away gently from the shore and went in a little distance and here came a shoal of herring."

"Have you got plenty of fish?" they shouted.

"Not yet," said Donald, for this much, it seems, he might say.

And they moved out farther. "Is that enough, Donald?" they cried. And again Donald said, "Not yet." So again they moved farther out to sea, and more herring came ashore.

"Is that enough, Donald?" they shouted. And once more Donald said, "Not yet." So they moved farther out still. And now came a huge shoal of fish, and the beaches were covered. And from out at sea came yet again the question, "Is that enough, Donald?"

"And," says the Seanachie, "Donald replied, 'Yes, thank God!' And down went the witches and were never seen again."

Ticonderoga

E VEN THEIR ENEMIES (and over the centuries they have
made quite a number) would admit that by the middle of
the eighteenth century Clan Campbell had achieved a position
of total dominance in the Western Highlands. From his capital
at Inveraray, their Chief, MacCailein Mor, from the first a loyal
supporter of the House of Hanover and by now Duke of Argyll
and Greenwich, wielded more real power than many a ruling
prince. Any potential adversaries, the Macleans for example,
who a century before had sacked Inveraray and burned it to the
ground, were either dead, in exile, or lying very low.

All around Inveraray was Campbell country. High above the
waters of nearby Loch Awe loomed the dark mass of Ben
Cruachan, and *Cruachan!* was the Campbell rallying cry. On an
island in Loch Awe stood the original Campbell stronghold of
Innischonaill, and in the narrow Pass of Brander, where the
River Awe flows out of the loch, the Campbells had in 1309
defeated their rivals, the MacDougalls, in a battle which marked
the beginning of their ascent to power. Here, on some higher
ground overlooking the river, stood the house of Campbell of
Inverawe, a Campbell chieftain of ancient lineage, who, like his
neighbour, the Duke, could (and constantly did) trace his
ancestry back to Colin of Lochawe, the founder and name-father
of the Clan.

On a stormy night in 1748, the laird of the day, Captain Duncan Campbell of Inverawe, a dark, strongly built man of forty-
five, holding a commission in the recently raised Black Watch, or
Royal Highland Regiment, was sitting alone at his desk in the
great hall of his house, trying to bring some order to his papers,

which, like most papers in the Western Highlands, were badly in need of it. A few peats smouldered on the hearth; the wind howled in the chimney, sending occasional smoky gusts billowing out into the room; and outside, the rain poured steadily down. Suddenly, just as the figures on which he was concentrating seemed about to balance, there came a furious hammering on the great door of the house.

These were troublous times. Barely two years after the Jacobite Rising or, as Inverawe would have called it, Rebellion, of 1745, the Highlands were still full of desperate men: marauding bands, deserters from both armies, fugitives from justice, smugglers, English spies, and Jacobite agents. With due deliberation, Inverawe rose from his desk and, crossing the hall, slid back the bolts and looked out. On the threshold stood a bedraggled-looking stranger, soaked to the skin, his clothing torn and stained with blood, his breath coming in short gasps. "I have killed a man," he managed to say. "My pursuers are hard on my heels. Give me shelter."

For the Highlander, hospitality to the wayfarer in distress is a sacred duty, and that this wayfarer was in distress there could be no doubt. Inverawe opened the door wide. "Come in," he said, "I will give you refuge."

"Swear it on your dirk," said the stranger immediately. And Inverawe gave his solemn oath, swearing on his dirk and, as tradition demanded, by Cruachan, the great hill in whose shadow he lived. Then, after providing the stranger with something to eat and drink, he led him through the silent house to a secret hiding place where he would be safe from prying eyes.

Scarcely had he returned than there came a fresh hammering on the door. Again Inverawe drew back the bolts and opened the door, this time to find a group of armed men standing outside. "Inverawe! Inverawe!" they shouted above the noise of the storm, "Your cousin, Donald Campbell, has been murdered. We are searching for the man who killed him. Did anyone come this way?"

For Duncan Campbell, only one course of action was possible. He had sworn to give the stranger refuge, and give him refuge he must. "I have seen no one," he said. At which the men ran back as fast as they could down the great avenue of trees up which they had come.

Deeply disturbed, Duncan Campbell closed the door, drew the bolts and again sat down at his desk in the hope that the dreary task of adding up columns of figures which never seemed to come out might help to distract his thoughts from the intolerable dilemma which confronted him. For, while he was relentlessly bound by his oath to give asylum to the stranger now comfortably installed upstairs, the equally sacred laws of kinship bound him no less remorselessly to ensure that his cousin's murder did not go unavenged. The fact that Donald, a born complainer, was not his favourite cousin, was neither here nor there. Blood, West Highland blood especially, was thicker than water. And spilt blood called out for revenge.

He had made little progress with his accounts before this ineluctable fact was brought home to him in spine-chilling fashion. The page of columns on which he was seeking to concentrate his thoughts was lit by a single, guttering lamp, leaving the rest of the room in semi-darkness. All at once, as he sat there alone, he became aware of a shadow falling across the page. Uneasily, he looked up. Standing at his side was a tall figure, ghastly pale and dripping with fresh blood. With horror, Duncan recognized the familiar features of his cousin Donald. "Inverawe! Inverawe!" declaimed the apparition in a high, piping West Highland voice. "Blood has been shed. Shield not the murderer!" And suddenly was no longer there.

Although he later made his way up to his oak-panelled bedchamber and lay down for a time on his great oak bed, Duncan Campbell slept but little that night. Whether he wished to or not, he could not ignore this warning from another world. Before first light, he sought out his unwanted guest and told him that he could not give shelter to his cousin's murderer. "You have sworn on your dirk," replied the other sullenly. And Inverawe felt ill at ease. He could not kill an unarmed man to whom he had sworn to give shelter, nor could he hand him over to his pursuers. In the end, the thought came to him that, halfway up Cruachan, there was a kind of cave of which he alone knew the position. Taking the stranger with him in the cold, grey half-light, he climbed up

161

to it and, without a word, left the man there to fend for himself. Honour, as conceived in the West Highlands, might not have been completely satisfied, but then, he asked himself, how could it ever be?

All day the question continued to plague him, and that very night it became all too clear that Donald's ghost had not yet been laid. Scarcely had he snuffed out his candle than he woke with a start to find the room illuminated by a pale radiance and his cousin Donald, pallid and bloodstained as ever, standing reproachfully by his bed. "Inverawe! Inverawe!" wailed the apparition (and this time the West Highland lilt was stronger than ever). "Blood has been shed! Shield not the murderer!" And again he vanished.

Sleep was out of the question. By daybreak, Duncan, with no very clear purpose, was already on his way to the cave. His dirk hung at his side, and he carried a pair of pistols, though what use, if any, he intended to make of them he could not have said. As it turned out, however, the question did not arise. When he reached the cave, it was empty. The stranger had gone, vanishing once more into the same vague limbo of men on the move, some seeking revenge, others fleeing from it. Making his way back down the hill, Duncan found such comfort as he could in the very human reflection that there was now nothing more he could do, one way or the other.

But he had reckoned without Donald. That night, he woke to find his cousin again standing over him, still pale and still bleeding, although somehow calmer and less severe, as though perhaps he had looked into the future and was satisfied with what he had seen there. "Farewell, Inverawe," he declared with a kind of sad finality. "Farewell till we meet at Ticonderoga."

To Duncan, the name Ticonderoga, if that was what it was, meant nothing. If, as seemed likely, it was the name of a place, it was certainly not in Scotland. No one he consulted had ever heard of it, and as the years went by time helped dim his memories of what he had endured. When not required for regimental duties with the Black Watch, he led the life of an ordinary West Highland laird, worrying about cattle, worrying about money, worrying about the weather, and worrying about people. Only deep in the recesses of his mind was he still conscious of an exotic name heard years before under scarcely believable circumstances.

By 1756, the British were fighting the French in North America, and there was peace of a kind in the Highlands. That summer, the Black Watch, orginally raised to keep order at home, sailed for New York, with Duncan Campbell, now promoted major, as their second in command. In June 1758, after spending the best part of two years in training and garrison duties, the regiment was sent north to join Major-General Abercrombie in his forthcoming offensive against the French, under the Marquis de Montcalm. General Abercrombie's immediate objective was the capture of Fort Carillon, strongly held by the French and strategically sited on the neck of land between Lake Champlain and Lake George. After a difficult landing and approach march, the British commander gave orders for the fort to be attacked on 8th July.

On the night before the battle, the Highland officers congregated in a disused mill. Sitting there, they talked of one thing and another with the nervous elation of men who do not know whether they will outlive the following day. After a time, their talk turned to the name of the fort they were to attack, Carillon, which came, someone said, from the musical sound made by the waters of the lake. "When we take it, we will call it Fort George, after His Majesty," said one officer, and another asked if anyone knew what the Indians called it. "I do," piped up the youngest ensign, proud to display his local knowledge. "They call it Ticonderoga."

Happening to overhear that half-remembered name above the general hum of conversation, Duncan Campbell, sitting by himself at some distance from the others, knew immediately what it signified. To a West Highlander it could mean one thing only: that he would not survive the morrow's battle.

The eighth of July dawned fine. The attack began at one in the afternoon. It went less well than had been expected. General Abercrombie, it appeared, had seriously underestimated the strength of the enemy's defences and the effectiveness of their fortifications. The attackers were thrown back with heavy losses. It had been intended that the Highlanders would be held in reserve, but, as the British casualties grew heavier, they could no longer be restrained and, rushing forward under a deadly fusillade from the French, they swarmed headlong up the earthworks, determined at all costs to fight their way into the fort. And this, with true Highland stubbornness, they continued to do until long after General Abercrombie, finally realizing his mistake, had given the order to withdraw.

In this disastrous action the Black Watch suffered appalling losses: eight officers and more than three hundred other ranks killed; seventeen officers and more than three hundred other ranks wounded. Among the less seriously wounded was Major Duncan Campbell of Inverawe, who had fallen, shot through the arm, while leading the assault with desperate disregard for his own safety. Having amputated the injured arm, the surgeon foretold a quick recovery.

But Inverawe knew better. Shortly after, a fever set in and on 16th July his condition took a sudden turn for the worse. That night, as he was lying in his tent, an officer who was with him saw him suddenly sit bolt upright, eyes staring. "I have seen him again!" he said, and fell back, stone dead.

When, many weeks later, official news of the Battle of Ticonderoga and of Duncan Campbell's death reached Inverawe, it came as no surprise to those who heard it. On the late afternoon of 8th July, two maiden ladies, the Misses Campbell of Ederline, had been taking a stroll by the shores of Loch Awe when, happening to look up, they saw in the clouds above them a battle taking place, saw the Black Watch as in their red tunics and dark, green, blue and black kilts they sought to storm the earthworks and were ultimately repulsed. And some days later, Duncan Campbell's foster brother had woken in the night to find an apparition of Duncan standing by his bedside, deathly pale, in full regimental uniform, while the red blood dripped from a wound in his arm.

Stewart of Appin and Campbell of Strachur

W HEN, IN AUGUST 1745, information reached Appin, green Appin by Loch Linnhe, that Prince Charles had landed in Moidart, the news was received by many with mixed feelings. To *Iain Glas,* Grey John Stewart, one of the natural sons of the Laird of Ardsheil, who dwelt in Glendochart, came *Domhnall Ban,* Fair-haired Donald MacIntyre, a gillie in the service of Stewart of Invernahyle.

"What is your news, Donald Ban?" asked Iain Glas.

"I have a secret to tell you," replied Donald.

At once Iain Glas rose to his feet and led Donald Ban to the middle of a large field near the house. "Now tell your secret," said Iain. "There is no person near us."

"The King has come ashore in Moidart," said Donald.

"Is there certainty as to that?" asked Iain.

"There is no doubt of it," was the reply.

"At this," says the Seanachie, "Iain Glas allowed himself to fall on the ground, and he rolled himself backwards and forward over two rigs of the field. He sighed heavily and said, 'Ochon! I am here now and my business thriving well at present, but it will not be long so. According to my promise, I am bound to rise with the Prince, but we shall never put the crown on him. We shall lose both our means and our lives by it, but that will do no good to the Prince.'" And, we are told, "Iain Glas made ready and went with the other gentlemen of Appin to try to put the crown on the head of the Prince."

As soon as the news of the Prince's landing reached him, old Robert Stewart of Appin, Chief of the Stewarts of Appin, set about raising a regiment of his clansmen, who, like their Chief, supported the Jacobite cause. At the same time, the Lairds of Achnacone, Fasnacloich and Invernahyle, who, as gentlemen of the Clan, aspired to commissions in the Prince's army, started to arm and equip their men. It was old Robert's intention that his only son, Dugald, at that time studying at Edinburgh University, should be Colonel of the men of Appin. But when informed of this, Dugald, whose mother, as it happened, was a Campbell, replied without hesitation that he would frankly rather spend the inheritance of Appin among the gay women of Edinburgh than risk its being lost striving to recover the crown for the Prince, which he knew could not be done. After which, he hastened back to Edinburgh.

Disgusted at the attitude of "the son of the Campbell woman," as he called him, Robert Stewart's first thought was to disinherit his son and in his place entrust the command of his regiment to his son-in-law, MacLachlan of Strathlachlan in Cowal, the husband of his daughter by another wife and a man well known for his devotion to the Jacobite cause. But to this the men of Appin took objection, declaring that they would accept no one but a Stewart as their chief; that they would kill Robert if he disinherited his son; and that if MacLachlan of Strathlachlan came anywhere near them, they would tear him to pieces. Disconcerted by their uncompromising attitude, Robert next suggested that his kinsman, Charles Stewart of Ardsheil, should be colonel, and him the clansmen, after due deliberation, agreed to accept.

It remained to put the proposal to Charles Stewart of Ardsheil himself. A big, fat, heavy man, Ardsheil at first showed little enthusiasm for the idea. In the end, it was his lively young wife Isobel who persuaded him to go. "If you, Charles," said Lady Ardsheil, at that time in an advanced state of pregnancy, "are not willing to become commander of the men of Appin, stay at home and take care of the house, and I will go myself and become their commander."

Having once made up his mind and put his affairs in the best order he could, Charles aquitted himself gallantly, despite his great weight. With Ardsheil as their colonel and Stewart of Fasnacloich as their captain, the men of Appin fought bravely for the Prince at Prestonpans, at Falkirk, and finally at Culloden, where they were in the forefront of the battle and where no less than nine of their standard bearers were killed, one after the other, defending the standard of their aged Chief and his absent son.

After what was left of the Highland army had dispersed and taken to the hills, Charles of Ardsheil set out for home on a large grey horse, known as MacPhail, which, the Seanachie tells us, was the only horse in the country capable of carrying him. At Ardsheil, he hid the silver and made such provision as he could for his wife and children. Then, after a narrow escape from the marauding redcoats, from whom his wife saved him by hiding him under a blanket, he too took to the hills with a price on his head, in the hope of somehow reaching the continent of Europe.

For a man of Ardshiel's bulk, a fugitive's existence was not an easy one. Because of his weight, he could move only slowly. The caves and hollows in which he tried to hide were too small to contain him, and, once parted from his faithful horse MacPhail, he had to rely on two loyal clansmen to push him up one side of a hill and lower him down the other. In the end, after innumerable narrow escapes and hair-raising adventures, he made his way to

Peterhead where, passing himself off as a wine merchant, he by good fortune found a ship to take him to Flanders. From Flanders, after an unnerving encounter in an inn with some of the British officers serving there, he finally managed to cross the frontier into France, disguised, it is said, as a woman.

With her husband in exile and their lands confiscated, Lady Ardsheil, summarily evicted from her home, nevertheless somehow contrived, with the help of loyal friends, to give her eldest son Duncan and her other children "such an education as was befitting for the children of the like of the Laird of Ardsheil to receive" before joining her husband in exile in France.

Once his education had been completed, Duncan, who, as Ardsheil's eldest surviving son, would ordinarily have become chieftain of Ardsheil on his father's death in France in 1757, made his way to America where, being well educated, he found employment as Town Chamberlain and Chief Collector of Taxes in the city of Boston. In Boston, he soon won the liking and respect of his fellow citizens. Although exiled from his native land and deprived of his inheritance, he still continued to use the style of Stewart of Ardsheil and was generally known by that name. In due course, he married the Governor's daughter, Ann Irvine, and settled down to spend, as far as he knew, the rest of his life in America.

A few years later, in 1776, came the Boston Tea Party and all that followed. By 1783, the British forces had capitulated and been withdrawn, and America, from being a British colony had become an independent country, strongly conscious of that independence. Not very long after this, it so happened that two itinerant Scotsmen, both from Argyll, arrived in Boston on a visit to America: General John Campbell of Strachur and Charles Campbell from Inveraray, the son of the local Commissary.

A leading member of his clan and a fine figure of a man, General John Campbell had had a long and distinguished military career. As a good Campbell, he had in his youth served under the Duke of Cumberland at Culloden. Later, he had fought against the French and the Indians with the Black Watch at Ticonderoga. More recently, he had played a leading part in many of the principal engagements of the American War of

Independence, finally withdrawing with the rest of the British forces at the end of that unhappy campaign. Now, having married and installed himself in some style in an elegant new mansion overlooking Loch Fyne, he was, with his friend from Inveraray, revisiting at his leisure the scene of some of his wartime exploits.

That, at any rate, was what he had in mind. But unfortunately for John Campbell, he was quickly recognized in Boston. As it happened, the former colonists had memories of him that were not entirely happy. "Notice was taken of the General and of Charles Campbell," says the Seanachie, "and observation made as to who they were. They were brought before a court of justice and it was ascertained that the one was a general and the other an officer in the British army. The Americans greatly hated the British at the time and the General and Charles Campbell were tried as spies who were going through the country in a clandestine manner. Sentence was passed on them as guilty, and they were condemned to have their clothes taken off them, their skins covered with tar, the surface of the tar covered with feathers, and fire set to them until they should be burnt to death."

A few days later, while preparations for their early execution were proceeding apace, General John Campbell and his companion were looking somewhat disconsolately out of their heavily barred prison window when Duncan Stewart of Ardsheil's wife, Ann, happened to pass by in the street below. "Mistress Stewart," they heard someone call out to her, and then, when she paid no attention, "Mistress Stewart of Ardsheil", upon which she at once turned round.

In the foreign and now suddenly hostile environment in which they found themselves, the name Stewart of Ardsheil struck a familiar, indeed a welcome, note. Though belonging to two clans between whom there had in the past been much bitterness and though they had themselves fought on opposing sides in the Forty-five, John Campbell of Strachur and Duncan Stewart's father, Charles, had known each other as fellow landowners in Argyll.

In his present precarious circumstances, a possible snub was something Campbell of Strachur was quite prepared to risk. And so, from his cell, he now sent a message to Ann Stewart, asking for the favour of a word with her, and a day or two later, Ann, who was a kindly woman, came to visit him in prison. "I heard someone in the street addressing you as Mrs Stewart of Ardsheil," he said, "and I wished to know where the Ardsheil is to which you belong."

"I," she told him, "am an American woman… I have nothing to do with that place. It is the land inheritance that should belong to my husband, if he had his own right. It is somewhere in the west of Scotland. I have never seen it. My husband was obliged to leave it and come to America, and I have none of it but following the name."

"I should like very much if your husband would come to speak to me before I suffer death," replied General Campbell. "He is my countryman. I have something to say to him."

"I do not think that my husband can do anything for you," said Ann, "but I will tell him about you."

On hearing from his wife of her meeting with the two prisoners, Duncan Stewart at once went to the prison and, on being admitted to their cell, shook hands with them, because, he said, they were Scotsmen. After they had talked together and he had learned of their predicament, he went home, much disturbed and also much moved. "They are my countrymen who are yonder in prison," he said to his wife. "They have come from the same shire in Scotland from which I came myself. My heart is nearly breaking for them, and I am disposed to let them escape, whatever may happen to myself thereafter. If you will steal the keys of the prison from your father, I will open the door of the prison and let them out. We shall put the keys back where we found them and it will not be known how the prisoners got out. But if you will not get the keys for me, I will break the prison, and I will flee myself along with the prisoners, and you shall not see me thenceforth. But if you will steal the keys from your father and give them to me, I will let the prisoners escape and stay with you."

Although not very keen to attempt stealing the keys from her father, who slept with them under his pillow, Duncan's wife, says the Seanachie, agreed to do what she could. Accordingly Duncan now went down to the harbour to make enquiries, saying that he and his wife were thinking of taking a trip to Scotland and were looking for a fast ship in order not to be too long at sea.

Having found what he wanted, he took the captain into his confidence and arranged for him to be ready to sail with the prisoners on board at the shortest possible notice. Next, he invited his father-in-law, Governor Irvine, to supper and plied the old man so heavily with strong spirits that in the end he was put to bed "jovially drunk". This gave his son-in-law and daughter the opportunity they needed. Before tumbling into bed, the Governor had indeed put the keys of the prison under his pillow, but soon he was so soundly asleep that, with a little skill and sleight of hand, his daughter was able to abstract them without his noticing. Once they had the keys, Duncan and Ann hurried to the prison and released the prisoners, locking the door after them and then replacing the keys under the sleeping Governor's head. After which, Duncan rushed General John and his friend down to the harbour and saw them safely on board before returning home. By daybreak, the fugitives were already well out to sea.

Next day, when the prisoners were found to be missing, there was a great to-do in Boston, and suspicion soon fixed on

Duncan. "If it is discovered that it was you who enabled them to escape," said his brother-in-law, a blunt Bostonian, "you will be tarred, covered with feathers, set on fire, and burned to death, so it is better for you to flee and leave the country as soon as you can."

Thus warned, Duncan "did not pass much time in making himself ready". Taking with him two of his children and what money he had about him, he secretly boarded the first ship he could find and sailed for Britain. His wife, he said, must follow later, when he had somewhere in Scotland for her to go to.

On eventually reaching the great city of Glasgow, Duncan had little idea what to do or where to go. But, wandering along a street with a child on either side of him, he chanced to pass the window of an inn at which, as it happened, were sitting General John Campbell of Strachur, who had lately been made a freeman of the city, and Charles Campbell from Inveraray. As soon as they saw him, they at once sent a waiter out to fetch him in.

Having no idea of what awaited him, Duncan was at first doubtful about going in, but the man assured him that he had nothing to fear from the gentlemen who were asking for him, and, once inside, he quickly recognized them both. Whereupon there was much mutual rejoicing and a lively exchange of reminiscences.

General John Campbell's immediate concern was how he could repay the man who had saved his life. Having a shrewd idea of how things stood in Scotland, he and Charles Campbell did not hesitate but instantly carried Duncan Stewart off in a coach to see their Chief, the Duke of Argyll. Finding MacCailein Mor at home in his great castle of Inveraray, they told him of their escape from prison and of the help Duncan had so readily given them. The Duke, an essentially decent man, was delighted. "What," he asked, "can I do for him?"

"You can go to the King and get his land back for him," replied General John Campbell, who did not believe in wasting words. And, not long after, the four of them set out in two coaches for London. There, the Duke quickly obtained an audience with King George III, who, always ready to pay heed to his manager for Scotland, agreed without much difficulty to restore to Duncan the lands of Ardsheil and, in due course, the dwelling house, which had been temporarily let. Duncan lost no time in sending for Ann and his remaining children from Boston and with them took up residence at Ardsheil. "And," says the Seanachie, "the Duke of Argyll was friendly to him."

Following the death without male heirs of the deplorable Duncan Stewart of Appin, latterly known on account of his heavy drinking as Duncan of the Gills, Duncan of Ardsheil became *MacIain Stiubhart na h-Apuinn*, Chief of the Stewarts of Appin, and in this role was enthusiastically acclaimed by his new friend, the Duke, and by his other neighbours, Whig and Jacobite alike. To this day his descendant still holds the Chiefship of Appin and, indeed, resides there.

The Water of Life

FOR MANY HUNDREDS of years, the MacPhunns of Dripp, a locality a little way inland from Strachur on the shores of Loch Fyne, were among the most ancient and respected families in all Argyll. When Mary Queen of Scots landed at Strachur on her way through the Highlands in 1563, it was with the Baron of Dripp that she and her retinue stayed the night, rather than with his no less noble neighbour, Campbell of Strachur, who at that time was in some kind of trouble with the Scottish Court. But circumstances change, and some two centuries later it happened that the Laird of Dripp had fallen on evil times.

It has long been a tradition in the Highlands that no honourable man steals sheep or cattle from a friend, especially if that friend is in a position to protect his own interests. But, in less enlightened times, to carry off sheep or cattle belonging to an enemy came close to being a duty. Indeed, many clans, notably the MacDonalds of Glencoe, did little else. It was thus that, as things became more and more difficult for him, MacPhunn's thoughts turned naturally to the idea of supplementing his diminished resources by occasional raids on the territories of any neighbouring proprietors not connected with him by bonds of kinship or friendship. For this purpose, he made use of an old flat-bottomed boat, drawing very little water, which he could run ashore at any suitable place in Loch Fyne, Loch Long, Loch Goil, or the Holy Loch. With a number of reliable friends or dependants he would land under cover of darkness in some carefully chosen inlet, drive as many sheep as he could from the surrounding hills down to the shore and on board his boat, and then, taking a circuitous route, bring them home and let them run for a while with his own flock on the hills above Dripp whence, in due course, they or their offspring would find their way to nearby sheep sales or other places where sheep and cattle changed hands for cash. In this way, he was able to keep up the numbers of his sheep stock at no expense to himself and thus maintain himself and his family in the style which he felt became them, a matter of no little importance to a Highland gentleman of ancient lineage.

But success made MacPhunn careless. He stole too many sheep from too many neighbours. Sheep were sold too soon after they had been stolen and too near home. Distinguishing marks were not always well enough removed. And the day came when the disappearances were not only noticed but traced back to Dripp, and the machinery of the law, such as it was, set in motion.

Though of noble birth, MacPhunn was not; as we have seen, possessed of great material or financial resources. To ensure acquittal of a crime which he had without any doubt committed, it was necessary for MacPhunn to pay lawyers and bribe witnesses, or at any rate to have powerful friends in the right quarter, the right quarter being Inveraray, the newly rebuilt stronghold of the Campbell Dukes of Argyll. Although in fact descended from a sept of the Campbells, the Lairds of Dripp had, over the centuries, lost caste and thus gradually lost touch with their noble kinsmen across the loch. And so it happened that when the time came and the sheriff's men arrived, the processes of the law were brisk and brutal. MacPhunn, despite his ancient ancestry, was bound hand and foot, bundled into a boat, taken across the loch, and thrown into jail like any common criminal. In those days, the penalty for stealing sheep was hanging. The evidence produced against MacPhunn in court was overwhelming and incontrovertible. Worse still, many of those whose sheep he had stolen were men of considerable influence, a fact that weighed heavily with the jury. After a short, simple trial, the judge put on his black cap and pronounced sentence of death, and MacPhunn, after a night in the cells, was taken out and hanged.

Highlanders have always attached great importance to a

proper funeral. Accordingly, once he had been hanged, MacPhunn's body was cut down and a message sent to his widow at Dripp, inviting her to come and collect it so that she might give it a decent burial with the ceremony due to a man of MacPhunn's standing. Draped in her widow's weeds and carrying her newborn baby with her, the Lady of Dripp, a dark, good-looking girl still in her twenties, now boarded MacPhunn's old flat-bottomed boat and set out on her sad mission across Loch Fyne for Inveraray. With her went one of her husband's most trusted henchmen, likewise dressed in sober black and profoundly thankful that in the course of the legal procedures his own part in his master's sheep-stealing exploits had not received undue prominence. On reaching Inveraray, he sadly helped carry MacPhunn's body down to the old flat-bottomed boat and having, with proper reverence, laid it out in the stern, set out on the long hard pull home across the choppy waters of Loch Fyne.

As she sat in the stern beside her husband's body, nursing her baby, Lady MacPhunn's thoughts went back over the years of their marriage. Though MacPhunn had been hopelessly improvident, and in his way a bit of a rascal, and though money had always been short, they had been happy enough together. If mostly mutton and oatmeal, there had always been plenty to eat. The roof under which Queen Mary had slept in more prosperous times was almost watertight. And a pot-still, hidden away in the cellar, safe from the visitations of inquisitive excisemen, produced as fine a malt whisky as any in the district — a whisky which for her husband had provided a welcome palliative to most of the problems of life. And now, still young, she was a widow, with a baby at her breast, facing an uncertain future, without her husband's unreasoning but never-failing optimism to sustain her in the trials and tribulations which lay ahead.

As the rower pulled silently at his oars and she sat alone with her thoughts, her eyes found their way back affectionately enough to the dead man's face, lying uncovered in the back of the boat. The hanging, strangely enough, had scarcely disfigured or discoloured it. There had been a large number of petty criminals to dispose of, and the hangman, without in any way skimping his work, had strung them up and cut them down one after another, as fast as he decently could. The corpse's neck, scarred by the rope, was mercifully covered by the plaid that had been thrown over him. The eyes were closed. The curly reddish hair which, as became his station, MacPhunn had worn lightly powdered, clustered as always close to his skull. His mouth, with the lips parted and, she could almost imagine, a slight smile on it, seemed as though he was about to speak to her. And yet she would never again hear his well-remembered voice or that merry, feckless laugh with which he had gaily dismissed the recurrent problems of their life together.

And then suddenly, as she looked at it, the body seemed to stir. It must, she thought, be the movement of the boat as it sped through the choppy water. She looked again, more closely. This time there could be no mistake. A kind of convulsive twitch had shaken the body as it lay there.

Life in the Western Highlands had made a resourceful woman of young Lady MacPhunn. She did not lose a minute. There was, as always, a bottle of home-made whisky in the boat. Spilling a sizable dram into a silver cup she carried with her, she quickly mixed it with some of her own milk and, forcing open the corpse's mouth, poured the nourishing mixture down his throat, while the boatman, resting on his oars, looked on in wild surmise. Again the body twitched, this time more vigorously. And then the unbelievable happened. Propping himself on his elbows, MacPhunn sat up in the boat. His eyes, gently closed by kindly hands not long before, opened wide, and a kind of gurgle proceeded from his throat. *"Uisge-beatha!"* he seemed to say, "The water of life!" In a word, "Whisky!" And his wife, a widow no longer, hastily thrust the mouth of the bottle between his lips, after which she took a gulp herself and then handed it forward to the oarsman in order that he too might refresh himself and duly welcome his chieftain back to life.

Thus it was that the little party which had set out sadly from Strachur a few hours previously to pick up MacPhunn, returned with him that evening in high spirits. Some hasty enquiries of the older inhabitants of the village elicited the welcome information that under the law a man could not be hanged twice for the same offence. Indeed, one of them recalled another happy occasion long ago, when the rope had actually broken at the critical moment, and the convicted man had gone scot-free.

Much relieved by the intelligence that there was no danger of MacPhunn being dragged back to the gallows, the party repaired to Dripp, to find the preparations for his funeral well advanced. Highland funerals are notoriously lavish. Without difficulty, the funeral became a feast to celebrate MacPhunn's return from the dead, and far into the night the good people of Dripp drank deeply to their chieftain's happily restored health. After which MacPhunn, his neck slightly dislocated but otherwise as good as new, settled down for many more years to the same happy, easy-going life he had been accustomed to. In his sheep-raising transactions he showed himself less enterprising, or at any rate more discreet, than previously. But the pot-still in his cellar was now joined by another, even more capacious device for the production of *uisge-beatha,* and the potent brew he produced, which he could rightly claim had brought him back from the dead, became known far and wide in smuggling circles as Old MacPhunn. Indeed, it is reliably reported that to this day a similar product is on sale at the Creggans Inn, Strachur, no more than a mile from where, as the map shows, MacPhunn's

Cairn marks the spot where he landed on his return from across the water. Both MacPhunns lived to a ripe old age and lie buried together in Strachur churchyard, under a stone neatly inscribed "Burying Place of the MacPhunns of Dripp".

The Widow's Cow

THERE WAS ONCE a fisherman called Donald, who lived in Tangusdale on the Isle of Barra. His boat was built on Barra, and his crew was one of the best on the island. Every year they were out fishing in March, April and May. Then, in the last fortnight of June and the first fortnight of July, they would go to Glasgow to sell their fish, fish oil, and general cargo.

Now Donald had a neighbour, a widow whose name was Mary. Mary had a cow but no croft, and before he left to go to Glasgow one year, she asked Donald whether he would let her have grazing for her cow on his croft while he was away. As soon as ever he came back, she said, she would take the cow off the croft, if he wanted her to. To this Donald, who was a kindly man, agreed.

It was a fine summer day when Donald and his crew set out at sunrise from Castlebay. "There was not a breath of wind," says the Seanachie, "and they were rowing and singing to themselves most of the day until they got a fine breeze in the evening, and then they put up two sails and she was going very nicely." Passing through the Crinan Canal into Loch Fyne and leaving the Isle of Bute to port, they proceeded up the Firth of Clyde and tied up at the Broomielaw in Glasgow, by this time already a considerable city.

When they had sold their cargo, which did not take them long, they started to lay in supplies of hemp for making lines, and hooks, and sailing twine for reeling in the hooks. They also bought tobacco, sugar, tea, a jar of whisky, and some clothes. Shirts were all they needed, for everything else they wore was made from wool grown, spun and woven on the island. "Next," says the Seanachie, "they took a day or two for themselves, and they would have been going to the pictures, only I suppose there were not such things to go to at that time!" Then they set out for Barra again, sailing down the Clyde, across Loch Fyne, and back through the Crinan Canal.

By the time the sun came up next morning, they had reached the top of the Sound of Mull. The wind was blowing east-northeast, a favourable wind for crossing the Minch to Barra. It had been a good voyage, and Donald was feeling pleased. "Donald," he called out to a member of the crew, whose name was also Donald, "fetch that jar of whisky." And he gave them each a dram and took one for himself. "Here's good luck to us, boys, and a good passage," he said. "And I hope that before the sun kisses the western ocean, we will be safely ashore on our dear island."

But the words were scarcely out of his mouth before the wind dropped and there was no breeze at all. And then suddenly came the sound of waves between them and Barra, and all at once a gale blew up from the northwest and they were forced to run for the harbour of Bagh Cornaig at the north end of the Isle of Coll.

There they stayed for the night. During the night the wind dropped, and the next morning they made a fresh start. But just as they reached the spot where they had been forced to turn back the day before, a fresh gale sprang up, dead between them and Barra, and again they had to turn back and take shelter in Bagh Cornaig. "Now mind you," says the Seanachie, "this was July, and they kept on trying this until in the end they decided to take the cargo ashore and put it into one of the barns of the men of Cornaig. And no one seemed to know what was the matter."

The weeks went by, and the harvest came, and still they did not get across. The potato lifting started, and still they were on Coll. By this time it was the beginning of winter, and still they did not get home. And now the season for ceilidhs started and, having nothing else to do, they went with the people of the island to different houses for the ceilidhs. And one night they followed the neighbours into a house where stories were being told.

The fire in the house was laid in the middle of the floor, with the smoke going out through a hole in the roof, and Donald himself was sitting close to the old lady of the house, Mistress Maclean. "She appeared," says the Seanachie, "to be very old indeed, and her hair was turning brown with the colour of the peat smoke." Outside, the wind was howling. Then, just as a man was telling a story, the dun horse belonging to the crofter came into the house, all covered with hailstones. "Oh, you dun horse," said the old lady to the horse, "is not the *cailleach* in Barra playing havoc tonight so that you have had to come home and take shelter under the roof?"

What the old lady had said to the horse caused Donald to think. "Mistress," he said to her, "I would like very much to have a talk with you."

"Well, so would I, Donald," she replied. "When the others go away, you stay behind and have a talk with me."

So, when the rest of them were ready to go, "Well, boys," said Donald, "I am not going with you just now. I know my way home, and I will sit here a little longer with Mistress Maclean."

"You are a kind-hearted man, Donald," said Mistress Maclean when the others were gone, "and you gave grazing to the cow of the widow, Mistress So-and-So. It is she who is keeping you wind-bound on Coll. But if you will follow the instructions I will give you, you will be ashore on Barra before sunrise.

"I am going to make a thread for you," she went on, and taking her *cuigeal* or distaff, she spun a fathom of thread and put a knot in it and then a second and a third. "If you do what I say," she said, "you will be ashore in Barra before the lady gets out of bed. Now go and find your crew and tell them to put everything in the boat."

Donald soon found his crew who, as it happened, were waiting for him outside. "Well, look here, boys," he said, "I am after having a talk with the old lady inside, and she made a *snaithean* for me, and if we do what she said we will be in Barra before Mistress So-and-So gets out of bed. You get ready the boat, and I will be down after you." Then he went inside to bid goodbye to Mistress Maclean, and after that he went down to the boat, and they set off.

"Well, boys," Donald said to the crew, "this is what she told me. When it was dead calm, I was to loose one of the knots and put up two sails. If I needed more sail, I could loose the second knot. But on no account was I to loose the third. 'If you do,' she told me, 'I doubt if you will ever smell the shore, for there will be a hurricane.'"

By now the wind had dropped, and they were obliged to row. Then they let go one of the knots, and a nice breeze got up. There was a late moon, and already the night was far advanced. When they came in sight of the little island of Muldonich, they undid the second knot, and the breeze freshened smartly, and Donald wondered whether he should reef the sails. But he wanted to be sure of landing before the lady got out of bed, so he didn't.

Before long they were in Castlebay, between Kisimul Castle and the shore. "Now," said Donald to himself, "I am going to test the strength of the witch in Coll." And he loosed the third knot. And as he did this, a sudden gust came from the northwest and cast the boat, the cargo, and the crew on the shore. "And," says the Seanachie, "if he had loosed it when he was on the sea, very probably Donald would never have been seen again."

As it was, he and his companions clambered out of the boat and went home. And when Donald arrived home, the widow was there, seeing to her cow. "Well, Donald," she said, "I am very glad you have come." This was too much for Donald. "Get out of my house," he said, "you witch that kept me in Coll since July last." And he swore at her upside-down and told her to clear her cow out of sight and clear out herself and no sympathy or kindness or comfort would he ever show her again. "And from what I am told," says the Seanachie, "the lady left the village and sold the cow and had no more to do with Tangusdale or Donald."

The Little Witch

ON THE POINT OF SLEAT on the Isle of Skye, a daughter and her father were one day working on a croft in the early days of summer, and lo and behold, they saw a ship on the water, up past the south end of Eigg. Immediately after, they looked again, and the ship was going to the bottom, and before they stopped looking at it, it disappeared out of sight. And he says to the little girl — she was only young — "I wonder," he says, "what was the matter with that ship?"

"I did that," she said.

"What?" said the father.

"I did that," she said.

"And who taught you to do such a horrible a thing as that, to founder a ship and a crew?" said he.

"Oh, my mother," she said.

Do you know what he did? He got a spade and killed her instantly when he heard that her mother did teach her it, and he killed the mother and the daughter, and there was nothing said about it. "Skye," observes the Seanachie, who was from Barra, "was terrible for witches in those days."

Sources

Dierdre of the Sorrows

Carmichael, Alexander, *Deirdre and the Lay of the Children of Uisne,* 1905

Campbell, Lord Archibald, *Waifs and Strays of Celtic Tradition,* Argyllshire Series, 1891

Diarmid and the Great Boar

Campbell, Lord Archibald, *Waifs and Strays of Celtic Tradition,* Argyllshire Series, 1891

Campbell, J.F. [trans.], *Popular Tales of the West Highlands* Volume III, Alexander Gardner 1892

Eilean Fraoch

Campbell, Lord Archibald, *Records of Argyll,* Wm Blackwood & Sons, Edinburgh 1885

Mackay, J.G., *More West Highland Tales,* 1940

A Sister's Curse

Campbell, Lord Archibald, *Waifs and Strays of Celtic Tradition,* Argyllshire Series, 1891

Princess Thyra

Campbell, Lord Archibald, *Waifs and Strays of Celtic Tradition,* Argyllshire Series, 1891

The Norse King's Daughter

Campbell, Lord Archibald, *Waifs and Strays of Celtic Tradition,* Argyllshire Series, 1981

Caivala of the Glossy Hair

Campbell, Lord Archibald, *Records of Argyll,* Wm Blackwood & Sons, Edinburgh 1885

The Isles of the Sea

Maclean, J.P. *History of the Clan Maclean*

SOURCES

Donald the Hunter

Campbell, Lord Archibald, *Records of Argyll,* Wm Blackwood & Sons, Edinburgh 1885

Campbell, Lord Archibald, *Waifs and Strays of Celtic Tradition,* Argyllshire Series, 1891

MacNeil's Return to Barra

Campbell, Lord Archibald, *Waifs and Strays of Celtic Tradition,* Argyllshire Series, 1891

Maclean's Return to Coll

Campbell, Lord Archibald, *Waifs and Strays of Celtic Tradition,* Argyllshire Series, 1891

The Last Hanging: A Tale of Tiree

Campbell, Lord Archibald, *Waifs and Strays of Celtic Tradition,* Argyllshire Series, 1891

Maclean, J.P. *History of the Clan Maclean*

Clara's Well

Campbell, Lord Archibald, *Waifs and Strays of Celtic Tradition,* Argyllshire Series, 1891

Campbell, Lord Archibald, *Records of Argyll,* Wm Blackwood & Sons, Edinburgh 1885

Maclean, J.P. *History of the Clan Maclean*

Duncan's Cairn

Campbell, Lord Archibald, *Waifs and Strays of Celtic Tradition,* Argyllshire Series, 1891

Campbell, Lord Archibald, *Records of Argyll,* Wm Blackwood & Sons, Edinburgh 1885

Maclean, J.P. *History of the Clan Maclean*

Macfarlane of Arrochar and the Laird of Luss

The Dewar Manuscripts Volume I, Wm Maclellan 1964

Cnoc an t-Sithein

Campbell, J.L. *Tales from Barra, Told by the Coddy,* Edinburgh 1960

The Skerry of the Blacksmith's Daughter

Campbell, Lord Archibald, *Records of Argyll,* Wm Blackwood & Sons, Edinburgh 1885

The Death of Red Colin

The Dewar Manuscripts Volume I, Wm Maclellan 1964

McArthur, Sir William, *The Appin Murder,* J.P. Publishing Series 1960

Stewart, John H.J. and Lt. Col. Duncan, *The Stewarts of Appin,* Maclachlan & Stewart 1880

Mackay, David N., *The Trial of James Stewart,* Sweet & Maxwell 1907

MacDonald, Mairi, *The Appin Mystery,* West Highland Series

A Substitution

Adam, F. and Innes, T., *Clans, Septs and Regiments of the Scottish Highlands*

Campbell, Lord Archibald, *Records of Argyll,* Wm Blackwood & Sons, Edinburgh 1885

Whyte, Duncan, Unpublished paper read to the Cowal Society, 1891

In a Sieve

Campbell, J.L. *Tales from Barra, Told by the Coddy,* Edinburgh 1960

Ticonderoga

Campbell, Lord Archibald, *Records of Argyll,* Wm Blackwood & Sons, Edinburgh 1885

Lauder, T. Dick, *Legendary Tales of the Highlands*

Richards, Frederick B., *The Black Watch at Ticonderoga,* New York 1911

Stewart of Appin and Campbell of Strachur

The Dewar Manuscripts Volume I, Wm Maclellan 1964

The Water of Life

Local traditional sources

The Widow's Cow

Campbell, J.L. *Tales from Barra, Told by the Coddy,* Edinburgh 1960

The Little Witch

Campbell, J.L. *Tales from Barra, Told by the Coddy,* Edinburgh 1960